D1226595

LIVING TROPHIES

LIVING TROPHIES

PETER BATTEN

DEBORAH STANCIL
Research Associate

THOMAS Y. CROWELL COMPANY
Established 1834 / New York

 Published simultaneously in Canada by Fitzhenry & Whiteside Limited, Toronto.

Designed by S. S. Drate

Manufactured in the United States of America

1 2 3 4 5 6 7 8 9 10

Library of Congress Cataloging in Publication Data

Batten, Peter.
Living trophies.

Includes index.
1. Zoological gardens—United States. 2. Animals, Treatment of—United States. I. Title.
QL76.5.U6B37 636.08'899'0973 75-40211
ISBN 0-690-01096-6

CONTENTS

PREFACE

A small zoo in California was the outcome of several frustrating years spent in attempts to find a suitable home for the private collection of animals I brought from South America and Indonesia.

During this time two zoos were built to accommodate these beautiful animals. Both won acclaim for their quality and the excellence of the livestock. Insistence on maintaining these criteria led to their eventual financial failure.

Five years later, without funds to continue operation, I was faced with the choice of disposal of the animals by sale to a dealer or donation to a city which could exhibit them and care for them properly. I decided on the latter course, and a phone call to the city of San Jose, California, in 1965 began negotiations culminating in construction of the San Jose Zoo.

San Jose is a large but culturally underdeveloped metropolis. A cursory examination of the animals' proposed home in Alum Rock Park convinced me that the care that had been lavished on the collection would no longer be forthcoming. Frequently vandalized, the park's pathetic menagerie had been the target of local humane organizations and tacitly ignored by city officials.

Negotiations with local government resulted in the choice of a new location for construction of a new zoo with my retention as consultant for its design and operation. Another year passed before the facility was complete, during which considerable differences between consultant and city engineers were ironed out.

The zoo opened in 1967 with administration by a newly formed zoological society. I was contracted as director and given full responsibility for professional operation of the facility. For six years the zoo was considered one of the best in the nation. Strict adherence to policies which I set up reduced vandalism and mortality to a minimum. Rather than typical window dressing for an amusement park, the animals were displayed in adequate, heated and cooled exhibits; the zoo grounds were well planted and maintained. No food was permitted in the zoo.

In 1972 it became obvious that San Jose citizens were not ready for a zoo. Admissions were decreasing while operating costs were rising; increasing reliance on city funds could only result in ultimate civil service administration, which I felt would lower standards in the zoo. I approached my board of trustees, and later city officials, with the recommendation that the zoo be phased out.

In 1973 the city council decided to close down the zoo and unanimously voted to return the animals to me. This transfer was consummated on September 15, 1973. A futile effort by a reorganized zoo society to build a new zoo in neighboring Santa Clara fizzled out, and I began efforts to place the animals.

Among the many U.S. zoos contacted, only one appeared appropriate for the continued care of my animals. At the Gladys Porter Zoo in Brownsville, Texas, Director Warren Thomas, DVM, was most sympathetic and interested in acquiring several of the rarer species. He assured me that they would be kept together and would find a "splendid home'' there. In the middle of December 1973 twenty-four mammals and birds left California for a new home. Unfortunately, I was at that time unaware of Dr. Thomas's unusual record and ethics.

In subsequent telephone conversations, Thomas assured me that the animals were doing well. Six weeks later I decided to see their new home and drove to Brownsville with a former zookeeper, Deborah Stancil, who later became my research assistant. We found that in their ''splendid home,'' five out of the original twenty-four were dead, six injured or mutilated by poor husbandry, and two traded to other zoos for species considered by Thomas to be of more use to his zoo.

This unpleasant discovery involved six days of evasive action and prevarication by the director, and prompted a personal investigation of other American zoos with subsequent decision to produce this book. The title was chosen as appropriate to the attitude many zoo directors show toward their animals.

From January through May 1974 every day was spent in driving to zoos all over the U.S. to compile firsthand information. Four months of depressing zoo viewing and photography confirmed that the majority of American zoos are badly run, their direction incompetent, and animal husbandry inept and in some cases nonexistent.

Upon completing the research and processing the 3,000 photographs taken on the trip, the following simple questionnaire was mailed to 200 zoos in America:

> We have recently completed a fact-finding tour of all U.S. zoos to compile data to be included in a publication this year. We would appreciate a copy of your Annual Report and Inventory.
> We are most interested in details on:
> (1) Number of Specimens

> (2) Budget Breakdown—staff, maintenance, animal care
> (3) Number of Keepers—male, female
> (4) Personnel Selection
> (5) Animal Acquisition—import, dealer, zoo
> (6) Security Provisions
> (7) Vandalism
> (8) Follow-up on Surplus Animal Placement
> (9) Mortality—mammals, birds, reptiles [most zoos seem to average 25 percent yearly]
>
> Your cooperation will be appreciated, and matters of interest pertinent to your zoo will be published in our book. We believe that this will prove to be of value to both zoos and the visiting public.
>
> Should you prefer to withhold such information, our observations will have to suffice. However, your views on such matters will assist in providing the reader with facts which we were unable to evaluate.

Replies to this only strengthened my feeling that something is basically wrong with the U.S. zoo and that it must be remedied, though it may jeopardize the careers of those responsible for the miserable conditions in which so many of our captive animals live.

Perhaps the 22,000 miles of travel and considerable time and money spent in research may improve the zoo animal's lot: the public should know the shortcomings of their zoos and take appropriate steps to initiate drastic and immediate changes.

INTRODUCTION

A wild animal's life is spent in finding food, avoiding enemies, sleeping, and in mating or other family activities. The pattern differs with the species but forms the basic way of life for all living creatures, including ourselves.

Intelligent people are aware that deprivation of any of these fundamentals results in irreparable damage to the individual. The absence of concern for captive animals, most of which live under conditions of psychological stress, is incredible.

Zoo directors theorize that captive animals "adapt" or "acclimatize" to the unfamiliar surroundings. They assure us that the zoo animal enjoys longer life and better health than its wild counterpart. Perhaps for a few of those that survive the trauma of capture, transport, change of climate, and unnatural diet this is true.

Regrettably, many of them do not. While it is impossible to obtain reliable statistics on mortality from time of capture, it is doubtful whether 50 percent of all animals trapped or captured in the wild live to see the zoo visitor. Those that possess a higher monetary value are treated with greater care; consequently, chances for survival are greater. Their "common" cousins are less fortunate.

Average zoo visitors are neither sadistic or moronic. Believing that those charged with and professing to understand the care of animals in captivity are competent to do so, they assume that these people know and do what is best for their livestock. Nothing could be more remote from the truth.

There are, of course, exceptions, but in America few zoos provide their animals the minimal conditions essential to their well-being; mortality is disgracefully high, and those animals that survive by sheer tenacity to live remain in miserable, small quarters for years to constitute a "record" for the director of the zoo. Should a pair of opposite sex fill in their long day by mating, the offspring are heralded as a "breeding success," and credit is given to the director for his astute application of suitable aphrodisiacs.

Worthwhile information on mortality and vandalism from zoo administrators is unavailable. Fortunately, zookeepers are often sufficiently concerned over conditions which adversely affect their animals, and provide valuable assistance in gathering material often at risk of their jobs. To these we acknowledge a debt of gratitude.

Replies from zoo directors in respect to deaths varied with the quality of the zoo to which questionnaires were mailed. Approximately 30 percent of the 200 zoos polled following our fact-finding tour contributed pertinent information. From a few second-rate facilities came petulant letters demanding our reasons and credentials for writing this book. Others arrived with what we can only assume were intended to be humorous responses.

The director of the Como Zoo in St. Paul, Minnesota, replied with his own questionnaire which threatened to start a mail marathon and provided a welcome comic relief from our miserable quest for a well-run zoo. Our questionnaire, which was intended to allow an official rebuttal of our findings, was helpful if only to confirm first impressions.

There were exceptions, mostly from zoos which are superior in caliber. Invariably, their directors showed concern over vandalism and mortality. They acknowledged the need for some follow-up procedure that does not presently exist regarding surplus animals which leave their zoo.

There is no doubt that improvement is needed in all of our zoos. How this improvement might be brought about depends on public reaction to disclosure of conditions in these institutions. Self-policing is not enough: action must be taken by concerned individuals independent of the political pressures to which some zoo directors are subject. Among these are humane and conservation organizations.

John Perry, self-styled naturalist and conservationist who joined the National Zoo as assistant director (a rather unorthodox switch), describes humane societies as "sincere but emotional people devoted to mammals and birds," and their attacks on captive animal facilities "astonishingly intemperate, laden with invective and threats of political reprisal."[1]

These groups on occasion may dramatize facts concerning animals, but there is no doubt that some of them are well informed and useful in bringing the shortcomings of zoos to public attention. Such action is unlikely to provoke criticism from zoos which are above reproach. (More recently, numerous self-acclaimed wildlife experts, who appear to recognize opportunity's knock, are exploiting the animals' plight to personal advantage. Perhaps some benefit to the animals may be incidentally involved.)

Government, whether federal or city, is slow to take action until public pressure demands it. Criticism of basic faults with publicly funded zoos is, to its officials, heresy. Until the American public insists, these poorly run institutions will continue to foster incompetence and reluctance to change, and exhibit the visible results of unqualified employees at all levels of operation. The place for initial change is in the zoo director's office.

Among approximately 150 men who supervise administration of the U.S. zoos are a handful of competent professionals. They operate a few zoos, some large, some small in size, with varied animal inventories.

To these people we must look for leadership in reforming our zoos, currently pitiful excuses for keeping wild animals in the name of education. Whether or not they will accept their responsibility by working together in an effort to share their knowledge and concern is speculation. The obstacles to be overcome before the incompetents will even admit discrepancies in their snug human sanctuaries are manifold.

Invariably, the well-managed zoo shows the unmistakeable stamp of a knowledgeable director. Not by the outward splendor of its buildings but in the consideration shown toward the comfort, both mental and physical, of its stock. To these few, size of inventory is of secondary import. Utilizing what is available to advantage, their animals are healthy and active but not overfed, diversion is provided for those that most need it, and visible efforts to improve husbandry and other captive-animal requirements are made. This may entail reducing the number of animals to make larger or otherwise more tenable exhibits. To these people we offer our admiration and recognition for doing an efficient job.

There remains a vast majority of zoo directors who are politically oriented, ignorant semi-professionals who by tenure, charisma, or their good fortune are responsible for the poorly housed, pathetic creatures we see in their zoos. Academic training is not of primary importance in the American zoo field. The Ph.D. or the high-school dropout may produce equally good or bad results. There are men whose training gives them professional status although their ethics belong in the gutter. These men readily prostitute themselves and their animals for personal advancement. Some are quite successful.

Directors of U.S. zoos have evolved far too quickly from grass cutter, salesman, dog catcher, and ice hockey player. It is natural that the zoological shambles they head should suffer chronic decay. These directors enjoy a unique advantage over their supervisors, as few people on boards of trustees or zoo commissions have a fundamental idea of zoo operation. With caution, they can err in judgment to the detriment of the animals times without number and retain credibility. Those who do, depend for any minor achievement upon zookeepers sufficiently concerned for the animals. (In most zoos, a few dedicated keepers are to be found, generally younger people.)

The incompetent zoo director has a hide like a rhinoceros and seems oblivious to his staff's feelings. It is generally recognized that the American zookeeper, ultimately responsible for animal care, is infinitely more important to the zoo than its director.

With this in mind, many incompetent administrators insist that all public relations matters (so important to professional failures) are handled personally. Any event in the zoo, not necessarily of earth-shattering importance, can thus be turned to personal advantage.

The zoo director turned TV star is one of today's most unpleasant phenomena. Semi-literate and folksy, these boors occupy far too much prime time. The public, imagining them to be experts, does not realize how infrequently they practice what they preach.

To these self-promoting individuals, many of whom are acquaintances, this book is dedicated in the hope that perhaps a cobweb-festooned conscience may feel a twinge and prompt a genuine attempt to clean house or relinquish control to somebody who will. Recalcitrants must be eliminated if material improvement to our zoos is expected.

To accomplish this, some form of licensing must be applied, and an evaluation of individual directors made by qualified experts (whose credentials must also be subject to investigation) uninvolved with any zoo. Should this become possible, 70 percent of our zoos would be directorless, in most instances an improvement.

PART ONE
THE ZOO STORY: FICTION AND FACT

1
THE ZOO'S PUBLIC IMAGE AND OBJECTIVES

American zoos are desperately trying to change their public image to justify a continued existence and ensure future supplies of animals for exhibit. Without these replacement specimens, the Natural History Museum with its silent occupants will quickly take their place. The zoo must give prompt and valid reasons for its presence, which in current form is in jeopardy.

According to the American Association of Zoological Parks and Aquariums (AAZPA) there are 305 zoos and aquariums in the United States. As they include animal dealers, ranches, museums, fun parks, attractions, barnyards, and zoo societies, a total of 185 bona fide zoos would be a more accurate figure. These may be large or small; owned by state, county, or city and usually staffed by civil servants; or privately financed. They vary considerably in size, presentation, and quality, and are visited by millions every year.

There are badly run zoos in attractive locations, and well-run zoos in bad locations. The common denominator seems to be insolvency. Widespread incompetence in administration and a hypercompetitive drive between directors often contribute to this condition.

Private zoos form a minority, and comprise most of the drive-through and marine facilities. Their survival lies in keeping the show stock healthy. Not subject to the disadvantages of bureaucratic personnel selection, animal husbandry generally tends to be better. A few pathetic roadside menageries remain in operation, all run by private individuals for purely mercenary reasons.

Virtually all of these animal exhibitors are members of the AAZPA, and enjoy varying privileges offered by that organization. The few remaining independent are tacitly ignored by the AAZPA and its members.

We learn through zoo publications (which are sometimes quite elaborate) that the world's wildlife is endangered by Man's depredations. There is some truth in their assertions; positive action to accompany the rhetoric, however, would be welcome evidence of efforts to improve matters. The following pages tell something of their publicized programs and goals.

Through insidious promotional feeding, Americans have swallowed a number of assorted fallacies that encompass a wide range of subject matter. Among these is the purpose for the zoo's place in modern society.

Zoos or zoological societies publish periodical newsletters or bulletins which provide information about the zoo, including social events, fundraisers, and "education" news. Their content is quite widely read, as mailing lists generally include zoos in other states.

It is only proper that San Diego, self-acclaimed biggest and best American zoo, should most loudly voice its contributions and benefits to wildlife. With prolific printed matter, the zoo is a master of the technique—appealing pictures of baby animals and semi-technical articles by staff and guest writers. The text carries an undertone of superiority not always merited.

San Diego's San Pascual Wild Animal Park has its own creative writers. On entering the pseudo-African park, patrons are invited, rather dramatically, to

Join us here . . .
. . . to contemplate the wild animals of the world and nature's wilderness.
. . . to strengthen a commitment to wildlife conservation throughout the world.
. . . and to strive toward Man's own survival through the preservation of nature.[2]

Deeply moved, they may pay admission and pass through the "largest outdoor aviary in the world" to the California-style authentic African village complete with African gift shops, African restrooms, and African snack bars to find with relief that the natives include little more exotic on their menu than hamburger, Coca-Cola, and popcorn.

Behind a window in a nearby building labeled "Animal Care Center," an operating table is installed and visitors wait hopefully for a zoological *Medical Center* episode—live! This does not materialize; the window dressing merely emphasizes the park's scientific associations.

A few "rejected" infants of assorted species languish behind glass, and bottle feeding may be demonstrated by an antiseptic nurse.

Intrigued by the profusion of Swahili names and conspicuous absence of Africans, the visitor is channeled to the "Wgasa Bush Line" monorail station. "White hunters" in bush jackets and sun helmets extract additional payment, and the tour begins. A monologue generously sprinkled with folksy witticisms by the driver-showman explains the purpose of the park, with heavy emphasis on its con-

"Pinioned" pelican. Routine clipping of flight feathers causes temporary imbalance and prevents long flights. For convenience of zoo staff, these birds are permanently grounded by amputation of wing digits. (*San Pascual, California*)

tribution to ecology and wildlife. Ubiquitous signs proclaim the rarity of, and uncertain future for, wild animals.

A well-prepared folder modestly informs us of the park's mission:

> The Wild Animal Park will emerge as a major animal research center. The Jerene Appleby Harnish Wild Animal Station for Medical Care and Research [quite an impressive mouthful] is dedicated to the health and observation of Park residents. A study of reproductive patterns of cheetahs is progressing successfully in an area separate from exhibits open to the public. Many research projects are contemplated.[3]

Cheetahs, currently, are fashionable. While they have been notably lax in producing offspring for zoo nurseries, births are becoming more commonplace. Oregon's World Wildlife Safari proclaims:

> Our six cheetahs from South West Africa live in a secluded habitat, undisturbed, to facilitate breeding and study.[4]

The cheetah breeding bug has bitten every red-blooded zoo director, and a striking example of their efforts and basic knowledge of this animal may be seen in the St. Louis Zoo. Conspicuous signs reading "Cheetah Survival Center" point to a large pasture where, during our visit, two cheetahs watched a miniature train crammed with adult adolescence pass their sanctuary, presumably trying to synchronize their survival program to the railroad schedule.

San Diego is more ambitious in its reproductive aims than most zoos. Its folder tells us:

> 40 ANIMALS HAVE BECOME EXTINCT SINCE 1900 [this probably means forty *species*]. The Wild Animal Park and San Diego Zoo have a successful breeding program for Przewalski's Wild Horse, which is no longer found in the wild. The Park will be able to provide other zoos with rare species, and perhaps return some specimens to their native areas.[5]

Their flyers assure us:

> The San Diego Zoo, now over 50 years old, maintains the world's largest collection of wild animals. Over 5,000 specimens of 1,400 species are currently on display.[6]

In addition, we learn from their *Wild World of Animals* that

> The Zoological Society of San Diego has a long history in conservation. . . . And during all the years of growth, special attention has been paid to those species labelled "Endangered."[7]

It is comforting to know that their advertising department has the situation so well in hand.

The guide for the Topeka, Kansas, zoo claims that "zoos are dedicated to the preservation of all endangered species" and shows "the official *endangered animal symbol*, as adopted by the Wild Animal Propagation Trust and the American Association of Zoological Parks and Aquariums."[8]

The Como Zoo, in its *Zoo Guide*, makes an attempt to enlighten visitors who might be sceptical about its fortunately unique presentation of animals, more fully described elsewhere. In an unusually fraternal gesture, a quote from Gary Clarke, director of the Topeka Zoo, is included.

> People see a sad faced monkey and immediately assume he's unhappy at being caged. But that's his facial expression. He wears it in the wild or captivity. Chances are he's used to being caged and he knows no other existence.
>
> The same is true of Bengal tigers. Zoo visitors always feel badly [sic] that these great animals are behind bars. But they are not really talking about the tiger any more than they are about the lion or monkey. They are seeing these animals as human beings; they give them human feelings—and this is totally wrong.
>
> In a zoo an animal has complete room service—every day. *All its needs and wants are taken care of*. In the wild, animals today are fighting for survival. They face parasites and other illnesses, they must constantly hunt for a diminishing food supply, and they have predators—including man—to contend with. The zoos of the world are the tigers' one chance of survival.
>
> *People should be aware of these things when they*

> *visit a zoo. They should accept the animal on the animal's terms.*[9] (Emphasis mine)

The guide further expounds:

> Under his [Director Fletcher's] management the animal collection of the zoo has been greatly expanded and improved. With his help Como Zoo has acquired such valuable and endangered animals as Siberian tigers, gorillas and orangutans.[10]

Our illustrations portray some of the new "acquisitions" expressing their contentment in their cramped quarters.

Some zoos are more realistic. Topeka unwittingly admits its contribution to the population and disposal problem of African lions: "Many babies have been born and raised in the Zoo," and states of another difficult-to-place surplus animal, "twin jaguars have been born in the Zoo every year since 1964."[11]

Phoenix, Arizona, emphasizes its contribution to education. *Arizoo*, the zoo publication, notes that "school groups and teachers head for the zoo each September. Some 150,000 per year attend the zoo's popular educational programs."[12]

Solitary confinement in sterile cells is commonplace in zoos. Despite Gary Clark's (Topeka Zoo) statement, it is safe to assume this monkey's unnatural surroundings account for this demeanor. (*Atlanta, Georgia*)

Philadelphia claims to have the oldest zoo in the country. Their *Philadelphia Zoo Animal Book and Guide to the Garden* demurely asks:

> HOW DOES THE ZOO RANK?
>
> Among the best in the world. It is famous for its fine and varied display of animals and for its outstanding record in keeping them alive and well for long periods of time.

Somewhat contradictory is the answer to this question:

> HOW MANY ANIMALS ARE THERE AT THE ZOO?
>
> Usually 1500 or more. *The number varies depending upon deaths and new arrivals.*

Continuing its quiz:

> WHERE DO ANIMALS COME FROM?
>
> Chiefly from professional animal dealers who *take all the risks of loss during capture and transportation.* Zoos only rarely send their own expeditions into the field.[13] (Emphasis mine)

The guide demonstrates the writers' profound knowledge of wildlife as we learn that "zoo Hippos open their mouths wide for two general purposes—to show belligerency or to beg for peanuts, popcorn, or other tidbits"[14] (or possibly to shout for help?).

A few zoos, in their signing and promotional materials, are intent on informing the visitor of potentially dangerous characteristics of their stock. "Biggest," "fastest," "man-eater," "powerful jaws," "strong talons," "treacherous," "wily," etc. form the major proportion of text in publications and brochures. A woefully thin, neurotic

European bear in the Pueblo, Colorado, zoo is labeled "KILLER."

The Como Zoo's guide book emphasizes its animals' inherent "vicious" traits. Jaguars have "been known to attack and kill humans," cougars "have killed and eaten humans," and gorillas "can easily kill an unarmed man." Siberian tigers "will readily attack and kill humans for food. But so few Siberian tigers remain alive this rarely happens."[15] In view of recent improvement in diplomatic relations, this may encourage Siberian tourists.

Emphasis on association with danger is common to most commercial animal shows. Ocean World, in a Florida brochure, invites the visitor to "see 6 different species of sharks savagely feeding," "vicious alligators," and for the less bloodthirsty, "performing 'trick a minute' porpoises and sea lions."[16]

Miami Seaquarium waxes poetic with:

> 60 acres of sea adventure. The fascinating drama of the sea springs alive before your eyes. The bold black-and-white form of the most fearless creature of all—the Killer Whale! . . . A size that can attain 25 or more feet and a weight of five to seven tons. . . . The announcer says, "It's man-eaters' mealtime!" Crowds line the rails of the world's largest shark channel. In more than a million gallons of filtered sea water you see monsters of the deep swim slowly by. You hope to see them slash savagely at a huge bait dangled from a bridge by a staff member.[17]

Sea World of Florida tells of its "commitments to marine research, marine animal welfare and preservation, ecological and educational programs" in a brochure that portrays an adult elephant seal (a federally protected animal) wearing a straw hat, bow tie, and "smoking" a pipe.[18]

The prize for incredible taste, however, must go to Marine World-Africa USA in Redwood City, California. Their flamboyance would leave Marlin Perkins speechless.

> Marine World goes wild! Six hundred jungle beasts have been affection-trained to live in open space, uncaged, with Marine World's life of the sea. . . . And you will go among them on a sea safari so astonishing that your mind will barely believe what your eyes will see. . . . There is nothing else like it in the world today. It is absolutely wild!

Soberly, the brochure reveals that

> Wild animals aren't wild. Ralph Helfer made it happen by loving animals. Instead of chairs and whips and guns, Ralph Helfer used affection. With affection-training he took the fear out of rhinos and the venom out of snakes. With patient, loving care he turned wild cougars into kittens and taught hyenas how to laugh. But really how to laugh.
>
> You will board a *primitive raft* and tour the jungles of the world. Look—it's a man wrestling a tiger! And over there—a giraffe leaps through the forest, his trainer astride his back.
>
> . . . Your raft moves into *open waters* and you look back at a mind-bending sight: there on the shoreline is the legendary white rhinoceros, 4,000 pounds of unmitigated terror, his trainer dozing peacefully against the hump on his back.

(The "primitive raft" is made of rubber and powered by an outboard motor which spews its wastes into the "open waters"/seal lagoon.) Shamelessly confusing elephants with airplanes, the visitor is invited to

> . . . *Taxi along jungle trails* high above the ground on an elephant's back or camel's hump.[19] (Emphasis mine)

We noted that all the felines' claws had been removed, presumably by Helfer's "patient, loving care."

As vultures circle over the careers of many zoo directors, records of repeated failures and mistakes are being conveniently shelved, and noble efforts are being made to join the "save-the-animals," "ecology first," "environmental" fanatics and other contemporary vocalists.

Forgetting or ignoring their formidable contribution to the disappearance of wild animals, zoos are preaching a doctrine of concern for those which remain, and talk of plans which will restock now barren territory by judicious breeding programs in their facilities.

Their publications show an apparent concern for the world's wildlife, though by their own avaricious collecting of mammals and birds (through animal dealers), which through incompetence, ignorance, and neglect die by hundreds every year in our zoos, they contribute substantially to the uncertain future of wild animals everywhere.

An obvious conflict of interest arises as continuance of the zoo in its present form, as well as the zoo director's career, depends entirely on further collection of zoo specimens—at last slightly curtailed by overdue legislation. Of prime importance to the zoo director is access to the remaining animals, and to overcome restrictive measures he must have a good sales pitch.

The valiant attempts to convince the American public that the salvation of endangered animals can only be accomplished with the zoo's help are a last stand. The zoos' public relations departments have created a super-species of their own—the abominable snowjob—to promote public acceptance of their remarkable theories.

2

A CLOSER LOOK

A cursory examination of the zoos' stand on conservation is convincing and impressive. Worthy of a closer look is their rather contradictory attitude toward animals already in captivity, their useful contribution to conservation and education, and benefits to zoo animals from research.

(*1*) *Conservation and Animal Dealers*

We are constantly reminded by zoo public relations people that wild animals are diminishing in number for a variety of reasons ranging from "expanding civilization" and "competition with domestic stock" to other associated rhetoric. Zoo operators prefer to ignore another major factor: hunting and poaching by collectors who supply the world's zoos and pet trade.

In filling orders from zoo directors, an animal dealer, using his contacts in foreign countries and their native hunters, is primarily responsible for the decimation of wild animals desired by zoos. High mortality of captive animals calls for frequent replacement and brings a steady income to the dealer. Good husbandry in zoos would mean bad business for him.

Dealers maintain compounds in the United States or overseas. In foreign compounds they assume some financial risks, although admittedly losses in such compounds are relatively low. The stress of shipping, unfamiliar food, and inept handling between country of origin and final zoo destination take a much higher toll than the holding compound overseas, where the animals at least have suitable food and climatic conditions during the first traumatic days of captivity.

Wild animal brokers need little more than an office in a major city, business acumen, and a telephone. Rapport with the larger zoos' directors is an asset. With little more than a fundamental knowledge of wild animals they survive in this competitive business solely by the heavy losses in zoos. They have no more than mercenary interest in their merchandise.

A book written by an established animal broker states that ten years ago he knew nothing of animals, and he cites several instances in which rare and valuable animals died shortly after delivery to zoos. While admitting some sympathy for the zoo director, no consideration is given for the animals' deaths. Throughout the book he frankly admits that the check for delivery is his prime concern.[20] As merchandise which can easily spoil, a high price is demanded. When an animal dies it is simply a financial loss to the underwriters. Understandably, insurance rates are very high.

A Miami dealer forwarded two sloths to the zoo in Lincoln, Nebraska. Apparently, personnel were not well acquainted with the nature of these animals and shipped them in a smooth-sided box with no hand- (or claw-) hold. The sloths' futile struggle to remain on an even keel was manifested in their arrival: dead from the ghastly wounds inflicted on each other in their attempts to find a solid handhold.

European dealers who initially shipped orangutans from Sumatra and Borneo lost 85 percent of the animals before arrival in port. Zoos kept survivors alive for a few days or weeks, as their knowledge of the specimen was rudimentary. The orangutans were exploited until death, after which they became freak-show and museum specimens.

These large, intelligent primates are still occasionally smuggled out of Asia by unscrupulous people. The capture of an orangutan is simple—the mother is shot and the infant picked up. Barbara Harrison, who spent several years in Malaysian Borneo, cites survival of such infants from capture to dealer at 25 percent, estimating that for every orangutan that reaches a zoo, three others die, increasing the possibility of extinction which they face.[21]

In Singapore, on my last visit, thirteen young orangutans waited shipment to the U.S. Stored in a filthy, flyridden compound in inadequate cages, several suffered severe intestinal infections. The dealer, an American citizen, told me that sailors smuggled them out of Singapore in suitcases, and lamented the increasing difficulty in finding suitable couriers, which he blamed on local government vigilance.

Fortunately for the orangutan, the U.S. government, through the Department of the Interior, has stemmed the supply of newly caught animals, which will automatically curtail trapping and necessitate better care of existing zoo specimens.

Zoo directors will be obliged to improve husbandry to prevent irreplaceable losses if further legislation is passed and enforced. There is no doubt that "endangered species" would be less so had they done this years ago.

There are enough animals in our zoos to perpetuate their existence. Instead of breeding indiscriminately, zoos must learn to keep their stock alive longer and promote protection and conservation of wildlife overseas—not in relatively small areas in America maintained primarily for the entertainment of tourists and monetary gain.

(2) *Education*

Without doubt zoos provide recreation and considerable entertainment. Feeding animals and watching shows or sexual behavior amuses some people. As a photographic background the zoo and its occupants are unexcelled.

School groups on their fashionable field trips routinely include zoos in their schedule, as teachers take the opportunity to socialize while zoo staffs police their charges and prevent mishaps. Social groups, church outings, and service clubs make considerable use of zoos; birthday parties held there are popular. Observation indicates, however, that the primary reasons for zoo use are only remotely connected with learning.

Large zoos offer tours, generally led by rather militant volunteers who distinguish themselves from the visiting public by use of bizarre uniforms. The tours may become tedious for children, teachers, and nearby visitors, as tour leaders are sometimes egocentric and not always well informed. Some zoos bestow the title "docent" (teacher) on these public-spirited educators. Teachers should be qualified and conversant with their subject: a few weeks of enthusiastic semi-professional instruction hardly make the title of docent appropriate.

Volunteers can be useful. When zoo directors exercise diplomacy in dealing with the more overbearing individuals, properly organized groups may be of great help. Their main attribute, though few zoo directors would publicly concur, lies in fundraising abilities. This provides therapy for the individuals and money for improvements to the zoo.

Movies, television shows, and other media available to children traditionally misrepresent animals. Children watching shows depicting people and wild animals, generally emphasizing a warm human rapport with lions, tigers, and bears, must wonder why Elsa's cousins live in ghetto conditions, or why the animals they are taught to preserve and protect should be captive at all.

Whether anyone derives lasting benefit by seeing wild animals from other countries in enclosures which inhibit their natural behavior must be evaluated without bias. Should one learn that the chimpanzee, for example, is a neurotic humanoid that cadges food from humans, and throws tantrums and excreta should this not materialize? Or that the orangutan, which by nature seldom descends to the soft forest floor, is a pathetic bundle of matted red fur in the corner of a tiled cell? Must the alert, gregarious California sea lion be represented by an animal, half blinded from filthy unsalted water, that spends its life begging for rotten fish?

In an effort to upgrade the zoo's image, staff members have been glamorized by titles (Educational Curator,

Male lion. Castrated, declawed, canine teeth ground away, and tongue amputated by knife-carrying visitor, this monstrosity survives to "educate" patrons of this Kansas State University sponsored zoo. (*Manhattan, Kansas*)

Visitors are urged to "Satisfy your curiosity, come see, feel" pelts of animals lost in Como Zoo. (*St. Paul, Minnesota*)

Dietician) which are intended to lend a suggestion of scientific involvement. In Buena Park, California, the Deer Park has carried this to extremes. Its staff roster includes not only Curators of Marketing, Maintenance, and Food and Beverages; but a Curator of Gifts and Souvenirs. People who are closely involved with zoos may recognize the new public relations gimmick, and few zoo employees seriously believe they contribute substantially to public education. The general public continues to regard a visit to the zoo as part of picnic fun.

Zoo educational material is generally ignored by casual patrons, as Americans are remarkably lax in reading informative notices. In an attempt to attract attention to explanatory signs, several zoos have introduced a semi-humorous system which is amusing and instructive. A childlike fascination for comic books assures at least a cursory glance from visitors.

Currently, zoo signs are a product of individuals who glean information from books and modify it to suit personal tastes, which vary considerably. Signs are expensive,

Surrounded by metal bars and on a concrete floor; the sign on African lion cage explains—"ENVIRONMENT OPEN PLAINS AND SAVANNAH." (*Montgomery, Alabama*)

but standardization would lower production costs. Preparation of authentic descriptive text on animals would be essential. European zoos have for many years shared basic signs and there is some evidence of a similar trend here.

Zoo directors should cater to the basic needs of visitors and overcome the urge to force knowledge on people who are too simple or apathetic to absorb it, while making reliable information available to those who want it. Admittedly this could deprive docents of therapy, but might inspire schoolteachers to do thorough research which could be passed along to their students before, during, and after their field trips.

When public relations staffs recognize that few visitors want to learn anything during their popcorn marathon through the zoo, and that serious zoophiles have already researched, elsewhere, animals that interest them, perhaps a system by which everyone profits will evolve. It might incorporate superficial signing for the casual observer, cartoons for the simple-minded zoogoer, and abundant information for the serious visitor.

Until these problems are solved, "educational curators" will continue to preach a personalized version of wildlife conservation to gullible laypersons. Meanwhile, in the same zoo, anteaters grind away their knuckles on concrete floors, orangutans and gorillas find temporary respite in unnatural slumber on slippery tiles, and giraffes and zebras move painfully on overgrown hooves in their paddocks. Substandard animal care will continue to identify the American zoo.

The zoo's contribution to education is minimal, and the regrettable truth is that most people, although they may visit a zoo, show no more than casual curiosity toward its animals. Years of hearing visitors call cassowaries "peacocks," toucans "frootloop birds," tigers "lions," and otters "beavers"—as well as frequent inquiries from certain ethnic groups whose sole interest in animals is mani-

Sign taped to tortoise invites up-to-five-year-olds to "Ride Me." Portly adult recreates childhood in another "educational" effort at Como Zoo. (*St. Paul, Minnesota*)

fested in the question, "Are they good to eat?"—has convinced me that people who wish to learn about wild animals are, like the Siberian tiger, a vanishing species.

While there is no reason to curtail a source of amusement, entertainment, or recreation which inflicts no strain on ecology, wildlife, or personal freedom, rare animals cannot be prostituted to supply family fun. The ultimate solution may be television; even the uncontrollable feeding impulse might be fulfilled by an exchange of snacks among viewers.

(3) Surplus Animals and Breeding Programs

There is a limit to the number of animals which may be housed in any zoo. Depending upon size, display space, and available money, the wise zoo director keeps his inventory within limits.

Reproduction takes place even in our worst zoos, and offspring eventually become too numerous to keep. "Donations" of animals from wildlife agencies are not uncommon, and odd individuals appear at the zoo with unwanted exotic pets which they imagine will be welcome and cared for.

Zoo directors seldom refuse these gifts, although they often become a liability. A general rule for acceptance of any specimen from an outside source is a signed release by the donor which gives the director a free hand as to the ultimate disposition of the animal.

People who "donate" pet rabbits, ducks, and chickens (which have generally outgrown their initial appealing baby stage) do not know that a large proportion of these little beasts augment protein intake for other animals. This practice is quite common, as people who decide to visit their ex-pets discover. It would be more appropriate for the director to explain the situation before accepting the animals, but few are willing to risk even a temporary breach of public relations.

In any event, all zoos are faced at one time or another with surplus animals. The zoo director's solution to this problem is simple and rather callous. To him, surplus animals are trading material and a source of additional income for the zoo. They may be swapped for others in neighboring zoos; sold to animal dealers, who dispose of them as they wish; or simply given away. The decision depends on what the market will bear.

This may not sound unreasonable or inhumane, and with a few stipulations need not be. Obviously, the zoo director cannot support every animal born in his facility, and another zoo may be looking for what to him is surplus. The fault in this method of animal disposal is that no zoo director appears to give the slightest thought to the future of surplus animals after they leave his zoo.

Cats, especially, tend to propagate under the least encouraging conditions. A visit to any zoo in springtime will confirm this. African lion cubs are so commonplace they are without monetary value, except to the unscrupulous dealer who will pass them off as potential house pets to any individual who pays cash.

In 1972 Lion Country Safari, Inc. produced seventy-two lion cubs in their two drive-through facilities. Since then, two more locations have been opened. Charles Chase, a Miami animal dealer, had fifteen lion cubs unsold in February 1974, and every zoo in the country seems to compete for a record lion birthrate, adding to the unplaceable surplus. (AAZPA listings showed twenty-five surplus lions for the month of February 1975.) The San Jose, California, zoo was unique in the successful incorporation of birth-control medication as part of the lions' routine feeding. This was initiated in 1969 with the aid of Dr. Wolfgang Jöchle of Syntex Corporation.

Unwanted by zoos, animals have been sold to dealers only to have their lives abruptly ended by a bullet on so-called "game ranches." Curtis Prock, of Donnelly, Iowa,

Birth control needed. Five lions share small cage (one is out of view). (*Alexandria, Louisiana*)

was fined $2,000 and given two years probation for providing wealthy trophy hunters—according to him, mostly professional men—with zoo-born jaguars in New Mexico. At least ten cats were killed, all originally zoo surplus animals.

Among the zoos which had, perhaps unwittingly, contributed to the hunters' pleasure were Chicasha, Oklahoma, and Southwicks's Animal Farm, New York. Alternate targets, in the form of black leopards, originated in Lufkin and Houston zoos, both in Texas.[22]

Released in a strange place after years of captivity, these unfortunate animals could have provided minimal "sport," and had no chance of escape. The $3,000 fee charged by Prock for each animal easily covered his overhead expenses and his fine. (He was allowed two years to pay.)

Entrepreneur Prock's business activities have reached

farther afield. In Belize, Central America, a local hunter and orchid collector, Jackie Vasquez, told me in April 1975 of Prock's profitable Central American safaris:

> We have plenty cats here. We will never finish cats. [Rather a familiar statement.] But Prock found it was much easier to cheat a man out of so many thousand dollars on a guaranteed shake [hunt] than to actually have the man honestly get his cat. Some [jaguars] come from New Orleans. Curtis used to fly them here with TACA [a South American airline]. He was buying the cats very cheap from the zoos.
>
> Sometimes the cats don't want to be free, but run back in the cage. The animals were afraid, that's why they run back into the cage.
>
> What he does is to send the hunter to fish in the river, send the jeep with his men and they run the cat up a tree and then he'd go get the guy and let him shoot it. He

Exhibited as "patriarch" of the zoo, this lion has sired countless cubs. Unable to walk or eat, it should be euthanized. (*San Francisco, California*)

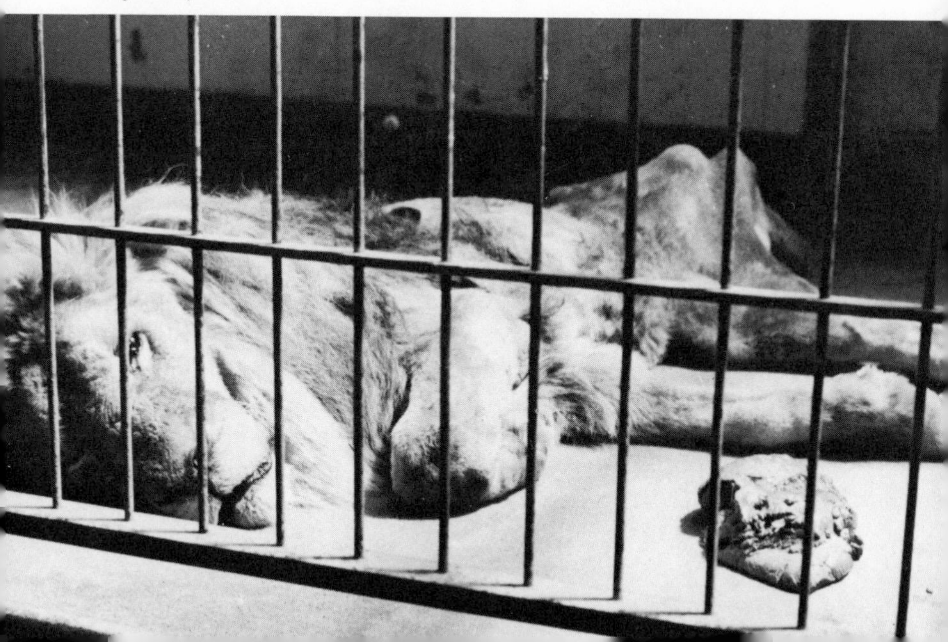

> gave a guaranteed hunt. You run all day and he put a cat in a tree for you. He screws you around the first day to make it exciting, then the other day you get your cat for sure.
>
> One guy came [from the U.S.] on the plane with the same cat he killed. He came on TACA with two cats, and one has a nail off, and when he catch the cat it's the same cat that's on the plane. The guy came on the plane with the cat.
>
> Since the Belize government stopped them importing the cats then he used to run them through the Mexican river border. The Belize government told Prock he's not to do it. They are going to check him. The native hunters complained about it but what can the government do when there's no men to check on him? They knew he was getting the cats—he was hiding them in the bushland.
>
> All of us [local hunters] was against it. He ruined the business. I reckon that's why Boone and Crockett Club doesn't come here any more—he was doing it too continuously.

Other U.S. citizens worked with Prock on his "guaranteed" hunts. Vasquez continued:

> Peter Tanner [recently deported from Belize] used to catch wild cats for Curtis. What Curtis and Tanner would do, he would send the boys all over his place to hunt, illegally, you know. And he'd take a hypodermic needle [with Prock's professional finesse, this probably was a tranquilizer gun] and they shoot it. Then put it in a cage, turn it loose, and the guys [Prock's clients] go shoot it.

Vasquez is a professional hunter and, like his peers, prone to overstatement. But there is no doubt that his statements were true, and they confirmed the few informative statements from Belize government officials, most of whom appeared to deplore Prock's activities. Nevertheless, the jaguars were imported with government consent.

It is difficult to believe that not one zoo director who sold Prock jaguars knew why he bought them, or that the Chicasha, Oklahoma, zoo, which helped house them prior to shipment, was not curious about their destination.

In Southern California the Inland Zoo at Norco enjoyed status as a bona fide AAZPA facility, including the right to purchase surplus zoo animals. For several years its enterprising owner, William Hampton, bought and traded U.S. zoo animals. It was not until 1973 that an alert member of the Golden State Humane Society stumbled onto a grisly find. In a fenced compound a number of crates were found bearing the names of many major zoos, including New York's Bronx, Los Angeles, Catskill Game Farm, and Boston. Further investigation revealed a trailer filled with the putrefying remains of dismembered animals and led to the discovery that Hampton and associates had systematically slaughtered surplus zoo animals, skinned them, and sold heads and pelts as wall trophies. Living evidence was provided by American alligators, found with jaws taped and starving to assure unblemished hides for eventual sale.[23]

In Eureka, California, the zoo director was elated at the opportunity to purchase a young Siberian tiger offered by the San Francisco Zoo at a bargain price—$25! Despite its ridiculously low price, sale of this animal was not an entirely unselfish transaction. As a cub, the animal contracted rickets from its low calcium/phosphorus diet and suffered consequent bone deformation. After frequent problems associated with this condition, it was euthanized in Eureka after jumping from its resting shelf six feet from the floor, sustaining multiple fractures to both forelegs.

Sale of this animal to inexpert zoo staff at this price was unethical and thoughtless. Small zoos cannot afford to keep such exotic stock. After this experience, Eureka Zoo exhibits only indigenous animals which it is able to maintain, and it is doing a good job. (Other older exotic stock—polar bears and African lions—were also euthanized.)

Two African lions, after ten years of captivity in San Jose, California's old Alum Rock Park menagerie, were sold alive to a Sacramento taxidermist for $20 each. During their lives, they were unmercifully harassed in their cage, and on one occasion set on fire with gasoline poured into the exhibit by carefree local citizens.

It would be unfair to suggest that all zoo directors deliberately inflict suffering on wild animals, or that they would knowingly contribute to such disgusting activities. Nevertheless, had a minimal follow-up investigation been made, many of these animals would not have been so inhumanely treated.

(4) *Research and Behavioral Study*

Psychologists, ecologists, and everyday animal fanatics have discovered that a wealth of exciting "firsts" await their miscellaneous talent in local zoos, as well as the possibility of generous grants from well-meaning foundation trustees and uninformed government agencies. Professional students of all ages have zeroed in on the opportunity and are living well on their stipends.

Major zoos are directly affiliated with colleges and universities, which, in addition to financial aid, offer a touch of authenticity to the educational image they seek. Intelligence tests, stock in trade of the psychology major, form the basis of research in the zoo. Animals which have been subjected to repeated frustration by budding Ph.D.s are easily identified in many of the larger facilities by their abnormal behavior. A great deal of time and public money is spent gathering information which is often available in textbooks ten years old.

Examination of stomach contents is another perennial favorite. Definite trends in diet established in animals do not discourage eager post-graduate students who happily sacrifice further specimens in the interest of science—and their future.

A seemingly endless supply of adolescent-minded researchers is joining zoo-based Frankensteins. Zoo directors, with authority to permit or refuse access to animals, are in a quandary. Denial may mean loss of funds from government or private sources; permission will rightly bring uncomfortable pressure from groups which are skeptical of the value of experiments performed on zoo animals.

Dr. Ray Young, formerly director of the Oakland, California, zoo and an excellent veterinary surgeon, has said that zoo research means killing animals to see what they died of. This lighthearted statement, unfortunately, seems an accurate summation of 90 percent of experiments on zoo animals.

In the New York Bronx Zoo several Demoiselle cranes were subjected to a futile experiment, later assessed by an independent laboratory which issued the following report: Blood samples were taken from the wing vein "while the birds were *lightly restrained.* [Emphasis mine] Subsequent to obtaining blood samples, the cranes were killed for purposes of evaluating any existing histopathologic changes in the vital organs."

Findings included some slight changes which "may be due to subclinical stress-induced cardiac damage sustained during the *forced restraint procedure* that was imposed while obtaining the blood samples." [Emphasis mine]

The unfortunate cranes were maintained "under the supervision of the Department of Veterinary Health at the Bronx Zoo," and were physically normal specimens.[24] Dr.

Young's comment seems appropriate. Whoever approved this "research" presumably feels that sacrifice of the birds was worthwhile or is not aware of what is happening in the zoo—in either case, irresponsible.

Mounting evidence points toward involvement between zoos and private interests in need of wild animals for experiments. The AAZPA meeting in Houston, Texas, was supported partially by the Institute of Laboratory Animal Resources of the National Research Council, which exists "to promote the procurement of breeding, husbandry, and *use* of laboratory animals."[25] Are they eyeing the American zoo as a potential source for future use now that government restrictions are making it difficult to import supplies? Obviously, the cooperation of zoo directors will be needed as well as approval of the AAZPA.

We cannot permit the use of exotic captive animals as tools for individual gain, financial or academic, without positive evidence that for every specimen "sacrificed" tangible benefit to its fellows will be a thousandfold. Either the zoos must be free from conflicting interests with the laboratory and animal supplier or cease their canting "conservation" and "protection" publicity.

(5) *Keeping the Public Informed*

The establishment of a favorable public image is important to the zoo and its director. Like toothpaste and toilet tissue, the zoo must remain in the limelight as much as possible to attract the elusive dollar.

Zoo publicity is generally handled by an ill-informed public relations employee, whose aggressive press releases find a spot in local newspapers. A small zoo's director may astutely use publicity to personal advantage. With help from the media, he may quickly become as familiar to the citizenry as the movie star or TV used-car salesman. A move to a larger or more prestigious institution is merely a matter of time.

Some current zoo administrators would have warmed the hearts of the deceased Barnum and Bailey. Thriving on any kind of publicity, these extroverts will try any means to get it. A few have chronicled and published their outrageous mistakes. Failure does not daunt these buoyant individuals who somehow avoid the untimely end they continually court. Their antics lessen the credibility of more serious colleagues.

The use of lions by Director Robert Elgin to control vandalism in Des Moines's zoo, while providing dramatic coverage in the local press, was asinine. A zoo director's flair for public recognition generally is inversely in ratio with his competence. Directors who have chosen to publicize their non-achievement operate (or have operated) our worst zoos and know least about animal care.

Nevertheless, a well-planned sales campaign is virtually irresistible, especially when accompanied by appealing photographic and live visual aids. At home, few evenings exclude a televised encounter with lions, elephants, or rhinoceroses. Viewers are lucky to escape with telephoto closeups of protesting shore and sea birds. Creators of TV shows still seem to be under the impression that Africa is the sole source of wild and exotic animals.

These creatures are shown impatiently awaiting the arrival of Marlin Perkins, Bill Burrud, and other supermen; a subsequent half-hour chase by Land Rover, Jeep, or helicopter; followed by roping, tranquilization, and tagging; with ultimate release to greener pastures, or delivery to that haven for the endangered species—the American zoo.

How these animals survived the monotony of their existence prior to the appearance of these intrepid showmen is a mystery. The same question might be posed with respect to their human co-stars. Perhaps we shall learn in future episodes.

TV Guide commented on the "high quality and continued popularity" of one series which persistently bombards us with salesmen saving wildlife from extinction. An intriguing statistic in the same article—"The weekly half-hour show [*Wild Kingdom*] is at the top of American Research Bureau ratings for syndicated series. Above *Hee Haw* and Lawrence Welk"[26]—provides a fair indication of its quality.

Our viewpoint is not unique. Peter Crowcroft, director of Chicago's Brookfield Zoo, cites Marlin Perkins's egocentricity, while Theodore Reed, director of the National Zoo, is more candid:

> I wish there were more zoology and less showmanship. Sometimes I get a little skeptical of the beautiful, handsome, suntanned Marlin wrestling with an alligator in the boat, and I think he's got to have a hole in his head. I mean, if he's really in all this trouble, what's the cameraman doing just sitting there taking pictures? Why doesn't he help Marlin instead? Oh well, if I did the program it would probably be duller than dishwater and no one would watch it.[27]

Dr. Reed's first comments express many people's opinion, but he apparently doesn't realize that bored TV viewers will watch anything: it is doubtful if anyone could be duller than Marlin Perkins. Promotion of his repetitive and often staged physical contact with wildlife is an imposition on the viewer. Hopefully, an animal will one day decide to tag him, and we shall enjoy it all live and in color.

Newspersons, in their eternal quest for the bizarre, flock with cameras to report a new zoo acquisition or birth, although flashbulbs, noise, and the presence of strangers may not be in the animal's interest while under stress. TV news reports recently showed the birth of a giraffe in San Francisco's zoo, unconsciously revealing the asphalt surface to which the baby fell. In another newscast, a newborn gorilla was shown shortly after birth with the comment that the director hoped the baby wouldn't be abandoned by its mother. Animal pictures of doubtful educational value (polar bears in bathtubs, apes drinking Cokes, and so on) are daily fare in summer tabloids. An escape, especially of a species considered potentially dangerous, receives wide news coverage.

There is too little reference, however, to animal losses in zoos. Quite frequently animals become alarmed by a thoughtless maintenance crew or other disturbance and will run into walls or fences, breaking necks or legs. A small news item may mention these incidents but usually emphasizes the zoo director's "heroic efforts to save the animal" rather than reasons for the mishap. The reporter, as unfamiliar with his furry subject as with modern zoo directors' survival tactics, often writes an article dictated by a public relations employee whose sole concern is promotion of the zoo. An "equal time" policy for the animal would reveal a surprisingly different story.

PART TWO
LIFE AND DEATH IN THE ZOO

3
ANIMAL HUSBANDRY

Instances of poor husbandry in zoos would fill an entire volume. This chapter deals with examples which illustrate common faults.

(*1*) *Neglect*

Excessive hoof growth is a common occurrence in many zoos and a direct result of negligence by zoo staff. Many zoo animals suffer the painful consequence of an incorrect floor surface or dearth of space, especially in the simulated goat "mountain" displays commonly seen in American zoos.

These may resemble rockpiles or castles and provide the aoudad, Rocky Mountain sheep, Himalayan tahr, or other hoofed animal with adequate, impressive vertical climbing space, but lack sufficient floor area. An inappropriate floor surface—often dirt, which in winter becomes mud—does not give the abrasive effect essential for maintenance of the animals' hooves.

A dirt surface is admirably suited to wild animals that can cover large areas while browsing for food. Confinement,

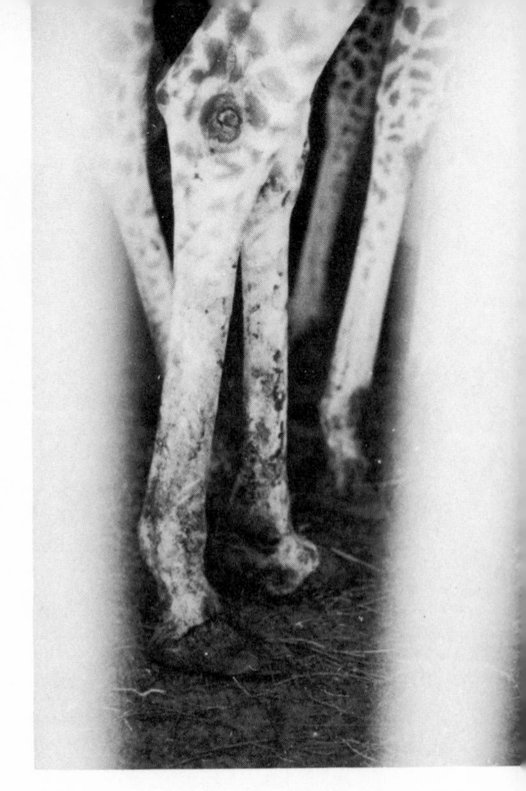

Floor surface combined with cramped quarters cause hoof overgrowth. Note untreated lesion on giraffe's leg. (*Colorado Springs, Colorado*)

''Endangered'' Hartman's mountain zebra immobilized by hoof overgrowth. Hoofed animals need abrasive floor surface and routine attention. (*Philadelphia, Pennsylvania*)

Aoudads cannot walk, much less climb their synthetic mountain. Animals' hooves need prompt attention. (*Racine, Wisconsin*)

with readily accessible fodder generally given in one spot, necessitates a little ingenuity on the part of the exhibit designer.

Stone or concrete may be employed, with a finish to assure adequate hoof wear in such limited space. Diets which accelerate hoof growth should be avoided, while prophylaxis in the form of frequent inspections and trimming would eliminate the need for subsequent heroic treatment.

During our visit, giraffes in the famous Colorado Springs Zoo were rather crowded (twenty-three in a medium-sized pen) and five of these with outgrown hooves moved with difficulty. Ibex in the Omaha, Nebraska, zoo showed similar signs of chronic neglect. Additional trauma was imposed on these animals by passage of a noisy miniature steam train which made the alarmed creatures run the entire length of their pen each time it passed. Taking the condition of their hooves under consideration, this must have entailed great discomfort. In Philadelphia, Pennsylvania, a Hartman's mountain zebra, conspicuously labeled "rare and endangered," had hooves overgrown to a point which literally prohibited movement in its pen.

Inquiries as to the reason for such poor husbandry drew noncommittal answers from staff, generally that the hooves were so far gone that the animal would have to be tranquilized, which would be hazardous. The head keeper of the Racine, Wisconsin, zoo informed us that their animals' hooves were trimmed twice a year. Our photographs illustrate the inadequacy of this schedule.

Rectification of floor surfaces for zoo animals could be carried out without excessive expense. Why such changes are not made at the first signs of hoof problems only a zoo director could explain. It appears that additional supervision is necessary to assure that such conditions are corrected promptly.

In zoos reputed to be our finest, animals that require highly specialized feeding and housing are often displayed on totally unbiological floors, devoid of simple factors that would make captive life more agreeable. Perhaps those which suffer most abuse are the Edentata, which includes the toothless anteaters.

These creatures normally spend a great deal of time digging and raking to demolish the termite and ant nests which may be above or below the earth. Some nests are built in high trees where only the more agile species of anteater, the tamandua and pangolin, can reach. Evolution has endowed most of the Edentata with front claws so long that they literally walk on clenched knuckles.

These active, somewhat nocturnal animals are at home in trees or on an earth surface. Keeping them on a hard, abrasive concrete floor in a glass-fronted exhibit is unbiological and inhumane. We saw only three zoos that displayed these interesting mammals correctly, on dirt or grass.

The greater or giant anteater occasionally climbs in search of food but normally stays on the savannah where there is an ample supply of underground termites. When provided an earth floor surface these animals thrive in captivity. In almost every instance, zoo anteaters had foot problems from abrasive floors in displays consisting of small concrete cubicles, where they not unnaturally sleep most of the time, as walking is uncomfortable.

Unable to assimilate anything larger than minute particles of food, anteaters suffer from the indigestable formulas prepared in many zoos and generally endure a short lifetime of diarrhea often ended by rectal prolapse. Homogenizing and proper constitution of their diet would assure complete digestion and eliminate these unnecessary losses.

In Topeka, Kansas, a tamandua in the large new rain forest exhibit paced nervously on a rough cement floor covered with improperly prepared and uneaten food. A commercial blender is unavailable for diet preparation. The cost of this new and quite impressive building's roof was $100,000, yet expenditure for a $350 blender is apparently

The other extreme of unsuitable flooring. Rough concrete wears these great anteaters' knuckles to the flesh. Digging animals need dirt-floored exhibits. (*Brownsville, Texas*)

Unbiological anteater exhibit—concrete floor, glass front, and solid walls. (*Washington, D.C.*)

considered by Director Gary Clarke an unnecessary extravagance.

The tamandua is seldom shown in zoos, and the pangolin is even rarer in captivity. Captive life has been tragically short for zoo pangolins due to ignorance of their requirements and consequent failure to provide them. Therefore they are not considered a "desirable" animal for exhibit: many have died of starvation after a few weeks or months in zoos.

These animals can live perfectly well as captives. Carrol Adams, in his privately operated Anteater Institute of America, Pasadena, has kept many different species of anteaters alive for years simply by applying good husbandry and consideration of their requirements.

(2) *Climatic Conditions*

Mammals, birds, reptiles, and fishes are comfortable only when they are able to select the conditions they prefer.

Wild animals can find shade, sunshine, water, or shelter at will, and move frequently to do so.

Captive tropical animals should be given what Zurich Zoo's knowledgeable director, Dr. Hediger, describes as a "microclimate." This can be easily incorporated into any display, and consists of artificial production of these conditions by the most practical means.

The U.S. Department of Agriculture's Animal Welfare Act stipulates that captive animals must have conditions (heat, cold, water, shade or sun) commensurate with their natural habitat. Either surprisingly few zoo directors are aware of animals' requirements and federal regulations, or the majority choose to ignore them.

Winter in New Orleans is cold and damp. There is no provision for heating the zoo animals. Director John Moore believes that animals should "learn to live with local climatic conditions" (also presumably, to die with them). Mr. Moore's unique theory of tropical animal husbandry may have originated in Baltimore, Maryland, while he was employed as assistant director.

A group of baboons are exhibited there in a filthy cage, its pockmarked concrete floor thick with algae. The animals are unheated and two had frostbite-amputated tails. A macaque in Roswell, New Mexico, was "heated" by a 60-watt light bulb in its box. This lamp, the attendant proudly told us, "goes on below 35 degrees." Baboons and macaques sleep in exposed steel barrels hung from leafless trees through the winter in Yosemite Wild Animal Park, where temperatures are well below freezing.

In Abilene, Texas, a modern zoo, an African porcupine and a lone binturong (a tree-dweller that naturally lives in warm, humid forests in Asia) were provided only with metal oil containers placed on the ground in pits exposed to a bitterly cold wind.

Scranton, Pennsylvania, zookeepers had forgotten to

Drive-through zoo monkeys sleep in icy steel barrels in limbless trees during freezing weather. (*Coarsegold, California*)

open an access door, and a leopard shivered on a shelf in the cage outside, its drinking water heavily coated with ice.

An emu, denied access to indoor sleeping quarters, crouched soaked to the skin during a heavy rainstorm in Jackson, Mississippi.

The only shelter for cheetahs in Toledo, Ohio's, zoo is a metal shed with two 250-watt heat lamps mounted in the roof. According to keepers, one animal had given birth to young in the shed, and the cubs had been successfully raised although the outside temperature was 17 degrees F.

In their natural territory, it is doubtful that any of these animals would experience temperatures below 70 degrees F. on the coldest nights.

In colder climates, zoos sometimes "store" birds and animals susceptible to cold in barns and basements. Care must be exercised to provide adequate space between cages. An infant Asiatic elephant, while inquisitively investigating a carelessly positioned adjacent cage in its winter storage quarters in Des Moines, Iowa's, zoo, sustained a two-inch lesion on its trunk from the cage's occupant, a jaguar. The unsutured wound healed, giving the elephant a bizarre appearance. It was jokingly introduced as "a new species of elephant" by director Robert Elgin. (Mr. Elgin is versatile: he has been a public relations man, amateur snakecharmer, and author of a book describing his incompetence as a zoo director. This book may one day be invaluable as a "how-not-to-do-it" manual for future administrators.)

American zoos provide ample proof that tropical animals can survive a great deal of abuse and discomfort. Directors who expose animals either show their ignorance, unconcern, and poor professional judgment.

Emu huddles outside closed access door in rainstorm. Doors to shelter should always be open. (*Jackson, Mississippi*)

Binturong (a jungle tree dweller) sleeps on floor in a steel drum at freezing temperature. (*Abilene, Texas*)

(3) *Feeding and Overfeeding*

Wild carnivorous animals generally have an endless supply of fresh meat for the taking. A square meal can involve considerable strategy and exercise or it may be enjoyed with ease. Most cats show a preference for a certain species and will shop around in order to find it. A great deal of energy may be expended in selection and taking of suitable prey. Digestive stimulation is provided by excitement during the hunt.

Traditionally, zoos have posted feeding times for carnivorous animals. The pacing of caged lions and tigers as feeding time approaches is a signal for crowds to assemble. Lions, especially, have rather poor table manners that fascinate visitors. Their food, generally placed hastily in a special slot or box in front of the cage, or handed to the animal on the end of a stick, provokes considerable reaction from the cat, and is finished in a few minutes. The visitor sees how "vicious" the lion becomes when eating; the animals satisfy a little of their hunting instinct, and everyone is pleased—with the exception, perhaps, of the unfortunate animal that provided the meal. It is doubtful whether the proximity of so many people aids in digestion, but the animals at least enjoy a momentary change of pace, albeit six days a week and at the same hour. (Zoo carnivores generally fast one day of each week.)

Progressive zoo directors have learned that feeding while the zoo is closed is easier on staff and animals. When the cats are fed in the morning, their metabolism ensures a more pleasing exhibit, as bowel movement may be timed to keep the cage tidy during visiting hours. Elimination of pre-feeding-time pacing by the animal, which can be distressing to many visitors as well as the animal, is another asset.

To provide the special choice of every meat-eating animal in the zoo would be difficult. Traditionally, the basic zoo diet has been horsemeat or beef, generally that which is most readily available. The slaughter of horses for captive animals is distasteful to many people, but is, regrettably, essential if we are to keep carnivores alive and well in captivity.

In recent years, the cost of meat has risen dramatically. Meat packers, who want to utilize more of their raw materials, have done a little research and proved that animals can remain healthy in captivity with less of the customary muscle meat and more of what used to be garbage. With the addition of readily available synthetic minerals and vitamin supplements, and a euphonious name, a feline sausage has been placed on the market. This product is high in protein (from non-meat materials) and incorporates necessary diet supplements. Feeding this prefabricated meat mixture only involves defrosting, weighing, and delivery to the animal—much more convenient than cutting bloody chunks of meat, adding essential minerals and vitamins, and losing quite a lot of meat in the trimming process, which entails throwing away inedible sinew and bone.

The average zoo director, always ready to find an easier way, has been receptive to the price of the new horseburger. This ready-to-go product is routinely used in almost all zoos, and the animals indeed remain alive and are breeding.

In the 1972 issue of Denver Zoo's *The Zoo Review*, Mr. Paul Linger, Assistant Director, acclaimed the new product, and stated that

> For many years, diets were basically a slab of horsemeat or beef, sometimes supplemented with vitamins and minerals, sometimes not. Of course, this did not work out as a balanced diet—seldom were additives measured, if they were used at all.

No explanation was given by Mr. Linger for the irregularity or omission of food supplements which are essential unless animals are fed offal with muscle meat, so we can only presume that the zoo's food preparation personnel were irresponsible or without supervision. Mr. Linger, in the same article (after the decision to buy the "new" food, and its subsequent use at the zoo), continued:

> The next step was converting the animals (and their keepers) to the new way of feeding. The cats were easily converted as the palatability of the new product was quite high, and seeing this, the keepers also readily accepted the use of the new food.[28]

Despite Mr. Linger's assertions, the food is unpalatable to wild animals, contains too much fat for the well-being of most felines, and has an unattractive appearance and odor. In zoos where it is fed we photographed globs of this substance on cage floors hours after feeding time. We watched cats, on receipt of this unpleasant imitation antelope, sniff disdainfully, then go back to sleep. Eventually, of course, hunger induces them to eat some, which is not an indication of high palatabilty.

Three lions (in Mr. Linger's zoo) that would commit mayhem for raw meat in close confinement lay asleep, surrounded by their meat substitute hours after feeding time. Here, for the keeper, the new food has one "advantage"—it prevents fighting at mealtime. The reason for the truce is the unpalatability of the food. Keepers in almost every zoo expressed a preference for feeding meat to the animals, including those in Mr. Linger's otherwise well-designed and maintained Denver Zoo.

The director of the Birmingham, Alabama, zoo was determined that his animals should accept this food, and decided that a leopard, who refused the substance, would eventually be obliged to accept it. In the course of this experiment, the animal died of starvation. Horsemeat is on

One advantage of "Zupreme" (synthetic food)—animals won't fight over it! Three African lions in small cage prefer to ignore their food; raw meat in the cage would create social problems. (*Denver, Colorado*)

the menu again for their remaining cats.[29] Such determination to change an animal's taste in food might be of psychological interest, but was hardly fair to the leopard.

A male Siberian tiger with an amputated tail in the Fort Worth, Texas, zoo vomited his meal twice in ten minutes. Ten pounds more remained untouched on the cage floor. Similar incidents were witnessed in many other zoos where synthetic food was served.

Unsuitable food is only a part of the captive animal's artificial existence. The tendency to overfeed animals, especially carnivores, is deep-rooted, and its effect may be seen in the shapeless blobs that represent the lithe tiger, lion, and jaguar. Informed Americans are gradually becoming aware that humans live healthier and happier lives if diets are adjusted to individual metabolism. Zoo directors may eventually recognize that their animals, too, need properly balanced diets and put a stop to the current trend of using them as garbage-disposal units. Until they do, we will continue to see paunchy, lethargic creatures in our zoos.

Tiger sleeps surrounded by synthetic food. Animals should be fed palatable food which they will consume immediately. (*St. Paul, Minnesota*)

Grossly overweight African lion reflects human ''kindness'' at Orphans of the Wild. (*Buellton, California*)

Billed as the biggest tiger in captivity, this animal is abnormally overweight from overfeeding and lack of exercise. (*Buellton, California*)

Food for captive wild animals must be palatable, nutritious, and of suitable quantity. The only major event in the zoo animal's monotonous day, feeding should remain a pleasure and provide jaw muscle exercise and stimulation for the production of digestive juices.

(*4*) *Great Apes and Monotony*

The behavior of anthropoid apes bears such similarity to that of humans that it leaves little doubt as to our origin. Comparative intelligence of the chimpanzee, gorilla, and orangutan is widely recognized. (Lower mammals, probably because of their non-human manner of walking, eating, and reacting, are less understood by the public and are often considered "stupid.")

Zoos have widely publicized breeding "successes" with captive great apes, ignoring the fact that these births relate to the animals' understanding of their biological needs rather than to human assistance. There is, of course, no reason why physically and mentally healthy animals should not propagate, provided that there is a pair of opposite sex.

One of the zoos' outstanding failures is their total misunderstanding of even fundamental needs for these highly sensitive creatures or reluctance, if they are aware of their requirements, to provide them. Mere possession of a large anthropoid for exhibit seems to satisfy most zoo directors, and their animals live in sub-Spartan conditions through intolerably boring years. Many have survived more than two decades in what may only be described accurately as cells.

Orangutans are perhaps the least understood of the great apes. The endowment of a rather soulful expression gives them irresistible, built-in pathos. The orangutan (Malay: *orang*—man, *hutan*—forest) is an introvert; intelligent, and unbelievably resourceful. The typical orangutan family rivals the Waltons in integrity, honesty, humor, and earthiness, while their sparsity of dialogue might be considered a bonus. Clothed in long auburn fur, and possessing perception uncommon in humans, this remarkable ape has escaped serious study to date. (For this comparative privacy it may thank the complicated bureaucracy of the Indonesian government and the relative discomforts of interior travel in Borneo. However, the demand for mass education must eventually engulf the orangutan, and its respite may be short-lived.)

An infant orangutan, orphaned not by parental rejection but by a capricious soldier's bullet in northern Indonesian Borneo, was adopted and for two years became the playmate of an American baby. Dubbed "Briggs," he quickly assumed membership in the household and surpassed his human companion in intelligence and agility.

Briggs accompanied his foster family to the United States with the blessing of the Indonesian government and was installed in the original Santa Barbara, California, zoo, where he rapidly became a favorite of visitors. Complete acceptance of his alien life and the natives of the city is typical of the ho-hum outlook which wild orangutans seem to have.

Like all young orangutans, Briggs was infinitely curious, and constantly amazed his human associates by his ability to make his way out of any confinement into which he might be temporarily placed. Chain-link mesh, Briggs discovered, could be unwoven at the right point, and he would often be found lounging near his exhibit area without leaving visible signs of his egress.

A heavy rope tied diagonally across the roof of his home to provide exercise would be found on the floor each morning, and replaced with equal regularity by his keeper. Omitting this chore on one occasion, the keeper returned later in the day to find the rope neatly tied back by Briggs. He frequently repeated this performance for visitors.

During his stay, he had a variety of temporary roommates, among them a Californian brown bear cub of approximately his weight (about fifty pounds) that had been salvaged by local fish and game wardens and given temporary housing. Briggs became quite attached to his ursine companion, which at night climbed into his sleeping quarters.

A problem developed, however, when Briggs discovered that intrigued visitors were always surprised to witness the short show he produced. When sufficient people assembled by his exhibit, Briggs would submit the bear to a rather thorough examination of the nature usually given in privacy by physicians. His obvious satisfaction to visitor reaction led to subsequent refinements in technique until performances were sharply curtailed by his "straight man's" transfer to Los Padres wilderness area, where he probably still recounts his unique experiences to skeptical fellow brown bears.

Another captivating facet was Brigg's selection of certain groups of people for special performances. He provided sophisticated adult entertainment, which he reserved strictly for the elderly ladies numerous in Santa Barbara.

For these privileged visitors, Briggs would carefully place his food dish in a prominent spot, pick up his bowling ball, deliberately position it in an appropriate attitude inside the dish, and then, to the astonishment of his audience, use the fingerholes for purposes the manufacturer had probably never dreamed of (at least in 1964). Making occasional visual checks for assurance of undivided attention, Briggs held his audience spellbound.

The meticulous manner in which Briggs produced his show typifies the ingenuity and dexterity of these apparently clumsy animals. A wealth of other startling accomplishments included in Brigg's repertoire were enjoyed by judiciously selected groups during the day. Outside opening hours, Briggs was most amiable with his caretakers.

Transferred to the Bronx Zoo at the age of four, Briggs is now a magnificent, well-adjusted animal, although his mechanical aptitude has cost the zoo considerable money in repairs. During a visit to the zoo in 1974, seven years after separation, he recognized and spent a long time holding hands with and kissing his former associate and foster parent.

Wild orangutans have been observed performing in similar fashion among themselves, demonstrating absolute individualism. Briggs is cited only to illustrate that captive animals need be neither neurotic or bored if they are prepared for captive life and provided with suitable playthings. Performing animals often enjoy an equally pleasant, albeit artificial, life largely due to their daily contact with trainers and work-day routine.

Zoos in general seem to be quite unable to understand this, and insist, as most zoo directors told us, on keeping the zoo for people rather than animals. This is a stupid and ignorant attitude. Visitors surely prefer seeing an active, apparently happy animal to a curled-up mass of fur in a sterile enclosure.

In Pittsburgh, Pennsylvania, an adult male orangutan sleeps most of the winter day in a pen which provides only seventy-two square feet of floor surface and is tastefully furnished with an old truck tire in which the animal subsides, surrounded by wall-to-wall leftover food.

Gary Clark, director of the Topeka, Kansas, zoo, abounds with public relations talent, and hit upon the idea of providing Djakarta Jim, a male orangutan, with artist's colors and paper. The ape's subsequent "paintings," innumerable signs informed us, have been sold to discerning art lovers for considerable sums. We watched a female decorate her exhibit with her excrement, and had we not learned from Djakarta Jim of the species' artistic inclinations we might have left the zoo under the impression that she, like most zoo orangutans, was bored and in need of therapy—rather than a budding artist making temporary use of local organic color medium pending arrival of more suitable supplies.

Chicago's large Lincoln Park Zoo displayed two adult orangutans in an eight- by ten-foot cage quite contradictory to the zoo's monotonous proclamations with regard to their animal care.

An orangutan couple shared a small barred cell in New Orleans, Louisiana, while a female keeper played with their infant, an undersized animal "rejected" by the parents and attired quite unnecessarily in diapers.

The Hogle Zoo, Salt Lake City, Utah, exhibits hairless orangutans which are either a new sub-species or have lost their entire pelage through friction or other housing-condition defects.

An adequately sized but very dark orangutan exhibit in Stoneham, Massachusetts, shows some knowledge and consideration for the animals. A female, allowed to keep her infant, pushed her baby in a rubber tub serving as an impromptu stroller to the male in an adjoining pen, who viewed mother and infant through the glass partition with paternal pride.

St. Paul's Como Zoo's orangutan sits sadly through the day contemplating the unbelievable chaos that is the zoo's main building. Stuffed to capacity with visitors accompanied by their dogs, skins of the zoo's failures on a table display staffed by enthusiastic volunteer female "answer men," sea lions, bears, hyenas, and a large tortoise (which was being ridden by an obese patron during our stay); this carnival is enhanced by the baby elephant brought up at intervals from the dark basement where it spends the winter. Heavy bars on the orangutan's cage are set too close to allow more than its fingers to pass through. The ten- by ten-foot cell was bare except for a shelf.

In the Birmingham, Alabama, zoo, a male orangutan slept in the corner in an attempt to hide in his barren pen, quite oblivious to the efforts of the keeper to attract his attention.

Cheyenne Mountain Zoo in Colorado Springs presents an interesting and spacious display containing eleven young orangutans which were behaving as well as young orangutans can. The fiberglass-covered floor was slippery and wet from a drinking fountain with which the animals squirted each other. We watched one occupant fall from a simulated tree with a dull thud to the hard floor; it is not ideal and should have a nonslip surface. The deep dry moat with a vertical drop of about twenty feet could be fatal should one slip over the unprotected edge. A simulated tree barrier at this point would provide economical insurance. Absent, too, in this exhibit, is parental guidance. Never would so many young apes be exposed to such conditions in nature, and although many natural hazards are eliminated, their behavior in later life cannot conform to that of a family-raised orangutan any more than an orphanage without adult counselors could produce well-adjusted adults. We can therefore only assume that it is an attractive show rather than a sincere effort to encourage natural behavioral tendencies.

The chimpanzee is an extrovert and has suffered in greater numbers than its two cousins due to its lesser extrinsic value and former ease of acquisition.

Traveling menageries contribute generously to our zoos' large number of neurotic chimpanzees, and living relics from these shows demonstrate traits which to even the least observant visitor must appear abnormal.

With few exceptions, chimpanzees in zoos are exhibited in small cages and many spend their waking hours kicking, banging, throwing excrement, and screaming at visitors and keepers alike. Often cages are in dark buildings and in close proximity to other animals with which the chimpanzee would naturally be incompatible.

Zoo personnel seem unconcerned and accept such behavior as normal—which, for zoo chimpanzees, it is. They view dispassionately the animals' demonstrations of their need for therapy. The abuse which most performing chimpanzees receive while undergoing training (frequently including the judicious use of a club) doubtless has something to do with their frequent anti-social tantrums as they mature in captivity.

A roadside menagerie decorates the Texas landscape with miles of unsightly signs proclaiming "SEE GORILLA" and exhibits an adult chimpanzee, labeled "Black Ape—Name: Gorilla," in a dreadfully dark cage measuring three by six by ten feet; inadequate even for a small monkey. His pitiful state of neurosis is apparently amusing to visitors.

In the Racine, Wisconsin, zoo, the badly cracked glass front of a dark enclosure bears witness to its occupant's state of mind. The Lansing, Michigan, zoo houses an adult male in a ten- by ten-foot cage in perpetual twilight; while in Oakland, California, three adult males, formerly used as research subjects, have a rather unnatural relationship usually associated with humans. Their "scientific" conditioning permits this simian *ménage à trois* to live harmoniously in their undersized cage—an intolerable condition for an equivalent group of normal chimpanzees. Ironically, Oakland Zoo prides itself on being one of the more advanced Californian facilities.

Gorillas seem less inclined to show outward signs of frustration in captivity and spend a great deal of time in meditation, one of the few activities available in zoos. With few exceptions, gorillas are housed in pens and cages as squalid as those of the average zoo chimpanzee and orangutan. In all but a few zoos, gorillas, too, last for endless years in such dungeons, suffering their monotony in silence.

Their comparative rarity and acquisition difficulties enable them to enjoy a few extras, such as a device on which the animal may sit and reveal its weight statistics to visitors. In the Omaha, Nebraska, zoo, an electronic arrangement transmits the pertinent information to the visitors' area by remote control. Of no value to the animal, this expensive equipment is apparently part of the standard zoo gorilla kit, and is seen everywhere in cages which deny their occupants even basic exercise space.

The primate building in the Cincinnati, Ohio, zoo, which rather immodestly proclaims its breeding record, can only be described as a concession stand which includes gorilla housing. Every form of edible is on sale, and balloons are gas-filled to order for the customer. During our visit an ample layer of peanut shells and popcorn carpeted the floor.

Lone male orangutan contemplates visitors through bars. Cage is bare except for concrete shelf where animal sleeps. (*St. Paul, Minnesota*)

The San Antonio, Texas, zoo displays gorillas in cages measuring eight by six feet with three-quarter-inch bars set three inches apart, further concealed by a glass partition. With few exceptions, even the best indoor zoo exhibits are little better than supermarket meat displays. In Philadelphia, these sterile pens have an unbiological addition in the form of a flush system which automatically sluices the tiled floor with water at desired intervals —appropriate to its men's room appearance.

A fine adult male in the Oklahoma City Zoo entertained us by vomiting and reingesting his food several times for want of something better to do. Very few zoos include any form of play materials for these animals.

Chimpanzee "relaxing" with metal beer barrel (empty) in his "habitat." (*Washington, D.C.*)

Gorilla in sterile tiled display is typical of captive apes in U.S. (*Erie, Pennsylvania*)

Some zoos, notably Bronx and Brownsville, are making definite attempts to alleviate their apes' monotony, but almost all others need both counsel and stimulus to make their charges' lives a little more pleasant. They are apparently unaware that solitary confinement is not ideal for any living creature.

(5) *Neurosis*

The different forms of neuroses in zoo animals all originate from an identical underlying cause—failure to fulfill housing requirements and provide mental stimulus. Nervous activity of animals in zoos generally produces repetitive movements of all or parts of the body, and tends to develop into distinct types of neurotic behavior if they are subjected to prolonged physical or mental discomfort.

The neurotic animal shows a definite progressive pattern. Individuals of a similar species show less susceptibility to neuroses than others; and apparently response to stress in captivity is not limited to the higher mammals, although their symptoms are perhaps more easily recognized. Pacing, generally parallel with open sides of an exhibit and usually after a fruitless inspection of the entire enclosure (including the highest points to which the animal may climb or jump), is an early indication of stress.

Failure to locate means of escape results in concentration on the front of the exhibit, where a persistent walk from one side to another may be initiated by the animal. A U-turn or loop incorporated into this routine produces a faithfully followed stereotype pattern.

An animal's tracks may be clearly seen on turf or dirt surfaces. It is not unusual for them to utilize only these worn paths, ignoring the total exhibit area. Such behavior may be observed in most species, but is predominant in hoofed stock and bears, possibly related to a natural tendency of these species to roam in continual search of food.

Primates show similar but three-dimensional patterns that may include chewing, fur plucking, total apathy, or a series of convulsive movements often accompanied by biting on a limb or extremity. This may be observed at regular intervals, in response to sudden stimulus, or terminally, in constant repetition.

The macaque monkeys appear to be prone to this condition. One of these in Midland, Texas, regularly climbs to a halfway point in its cage, shakes furiously on the wire, and returns quietly to the floor. This cycle is repeated in detail and at exactly the same place.

El Paso, Texas, exhibited a guenon monkey with a nervous problem inducing the animal to repeatedly circle and scratch. A lone lion-tailed macaque in Tucson, Arizona, demonstrated an almost identical movement.

Ron's Children's Zoo in Riverside, California, offered a more sophisticated show with a Celebes ape which repeatedly acted in pantomime as though stung by a bee—plucking, biting, and scratching the same spot on its arm and hand. The owner informed us this habit had been acquired some *five years* previously.

Anthropoid apes showing neurotic behavior are as familiar to zoogoers as the head-swaying elephant: many visitors believe these to be the animals' normal traits.

Polar bears often show their neuroses by head nodding, bar chewing, and pacing with abrupt halts. The polar bear in the Central Park Zoo, New York—alone since a companion was shot and killed by police after an inebriate put his arm through the bars of the exhibit—demonstrates this pattern to perfection.

An artificially induced neurosis may be seen in Springfield, Massachusetts, where an incident almost identical to that in Central Park left a polar bear alive but with a bullet in its head. The animal suffers periodic fits of screaming, probably from cranial pressure.

The polar bear in Jackson, Mississippi, adds a little to the usual neurotic behavior with a gruesome water ballet in which it enters the small pool on one side, leans back, swims under water, touches a protruding rock on the side of the pool with its nose, swims to the opposite side, exits, and repeats. Its repeated performances indicate this to be involuntary.

The National Zoo, Washington, D.C., exhibits an Indian rhinoceros whose nervous head swaying has completely removed its two horns from friction with the badly positioned (vertical) bars and the abrasive wall next to the access door which leads to its outside pen.

In New York's Buffalo Zoo a cage contained two black

Jaguar displays stereotyped movement, involving pacing, throwing head back, and touching wall of cage with nose. This is repeated throughout daylight hours. (*New Orleans, Louisiana*)

Coatimundi shows identical pattern in Tropic Gardens Zoo. (*Phoenix, Arizona*)

leopards that systematically chewed tufts of fur from their bodies.

Phoenix, Arizona's, zoo houses mountain lions, wolves, and bobcats in glass-fronted pens devoid of shelter and admitting far too much sunlight for these shy creatures. Their early signs of stereotyped pacing could be relieved by placement of a screen behind which they could rest, unobserved, in the exhibit.

The Tasmanian devil, a small badgerlike creature from New Zealand, is displayed at Cincinnati's zoo in a small cage with a concrete floor totally unsuited to this burrowing animal. It entertains visitors with perpetual motion in a three-foot circle. An equally neurotic coatimundi may be found in Phoenix's Tropic Gardens Zoo, where it spends a great deal of time on one side of the cage performing a routine pattern which includes a typical spasmodic backward jerking of its head.

New Orleans offers, with its old-world charm and excellent creole food, one of the worst zoos in the country. In this rundown Bastille, a male jaguar in a filthy, small, ghastly colored cage paced, stood up at one corner, threw back its head convulsively, and repeated the performance throughout our visit. This pathetic animal's gyrations made our walk to the exit, through waterholes in the pavement, seem relatively pleasant.

Quite apart from the distressing spectacle presented zoo patrons, these animals demonstrate an urgent need for therapy but are too often ignored by an unenlightened staff. All through the country, animals show inability to cope with life under conditions beyond their control while no attempt is made to prevent or alleviate these problems.

Reasons for neurotic behavior are manifold, but contributing causes in zoo animals include stress from capture (generally associated with adult animals), improper floor surfaces, teasing and other public interference, begging for food, too much or too little light, excessive noise, and other factors associated with captive life. Failure by zoos to provide adequate sleeping or hiding places for animals results in frustration and neurosis. Proximity of visitors under certain conditions (animals with young, etc.) often results in abnormal behavior.

Change of residence or introduction of compatible animals may relieve the early signs of neurosis; euthanasia alone can eliminate the deep-rooted stereotyped pattern in captive animals.

(6) *Marine Mammals*

Although a major attraction in the zoo, sea lions and seals have a brief captive life. Commonly displayed are Californian sea lions, and more than any other these animals are exploited to amuse and entertain in return for food which is quite often of poor quality and in some instances synthetic.

This popular zoo and circus animal deserves serious research into its behavior and captive requirements: of all animals commonly exhibited in zoos these must be the least understood. Their life is radically shortened in zoos by poor husbandry. Perhaps the sea lion's on-the-hoof (or flipper) value of about $125 accounts for this.

Ocean water, the marine mammal's natural environment, contains salt and trace minerals essential to the sea lion's well-being. The animals, as well as most sea birds and marine life, drink sea water regularly, and have evolved a systematic means of eliminating excess salt.

Naturally gregarious, they roam or rest in fairly large groups which are often segregated by sex during certain periods. Varying with the species, some spend more time out of the water than others, often several weeks. A heavy layer of fat insulates all seals from the cold, and to some extent heat; and while this layer is maintained by consumption of sufficient food, the animal can also endure long fasting periods, living meanwhile from its own fat storage.

Accustomed in the wild to feeding when and on what they prefer, which is always fresh, it is not surprising that captive animals do not thrive on food which may be thrown to them once or twice a day at the convenience of a keeper, or given one at a time by visitors who include with their offering any bacteria present on their hands. The fish, fed by either visitor or keeper, may have been frozen for six months or be an ersatz product which looks and tastes like synthetic rubber and does little to promote longevity. Furthermore, when fish is fed, the zoo diet generally consists of one variety of fish—quite different from free choice of food which the animal would eat in the ocean. Varying with seasons, seals take many different species. Each of these fish may provide nutrients peculiar to its kind.

The synthetic seal food produced and given a pleasant-sounding name by the manufacturers is composed of dehydrated fish flour and cereal products unlikely to be part of wild marine mammals' daily diet. It is never accepted readily, any more than a similar synthetic meat product is taken by the carnivores. Many marine mammals refuse this substitute despite lengthy periods of starvation. Apart from such food's unpalatability, many zoo seals have demonstrated stomach or intestinal disorders which are difficult to explain at autopsy.

In addition to the inappropriate diet offered captive seals, these animals are always kept in fresh water which is generally dirty and stale, with a liberal surface coating of debris. Urinating and defecating in this water, they are also obliged to drink it.

Many deaths may be attributed to foreign bodies swallowed by seals. Their short lives in captivity are spent begging, while visitors delight in their "friendly" gestures and throw any surplus material to attract their attention.

Fungus on sea lions in underground storage quarters. Salt water successfully clears up similar infections in this species. (*St. Paul, Minnesota*)

Sea lion with chronic photophobia from dirty, unsalted water. (*San Francisco, California*)

This is often ingested by hungry animals. Tennis balls, plastic toys, bottles, razor blades, jagged stones, pencils, and screwdrivers are among the miscellaneous items recovered at postmortem.

In the St. Paul, Minnesota, zoo, two young Californian sea lions share a small indoor pool in the building that houses most of the caged animals. Below this is a dark basement where two less fortunate off-display sea lions showed chronic skin problems, either fungus growth or, possibly, chlorine burns. Front and rear flippers were bereft of fur. Any medical treatment being provided these animals showed no sign of success, although similar fungus on seals kept in fresh water disappeared shortly after the animals were returned to the sea where they could be observed (Coast Guard Pier, Monterey, California).

At the San Antonio, Texas, zoo, we noticed a very thin female sea lion in an exhibit. When questioned in regard to the sea lion's condition and photophobia, which forced the animal to close its eyes to avoid the bright sun, the supervisor of mammals curtly informed us that she "had something in her eye." In answer to further inquiries as to the use of salt water in an effort to improve her condition, we were told, quite incorrectly, that the pool already contained sufficient salt. If the director of this zoo is aware of the need for salt water, action should be taken to incorporate it in daily husbandry.*

Zoos must discontinue keeping marine mammals under circumstances which shorten their lives. Marine aquariums are the only places in which these animals enjoy nearly a normal lifespan in clean sea water with a variety of fresh or properly thawed and washed frozen fish. Such institutions,

* We were unable to see the director as it was Saturday afternoon, but we did take photographs in his office, thanks to his secretary's desire to fulfill her public relations responsibilities. The same lady told us, while we viewed wall trophies from the zoo, that a lion formerly used as an office rug had presented a problem—she was continually tripping over its head.

almost all of them commercially operated, concur that these basic needs must be met if marine mammals are to thrive.

As an exception to this rule, we watched a number of sea lions at "Marineworld," Redwood City, California, swim in a "lagoon" containing water so opaque that it successfully inhibited viewing of more than the animals' heads. This fluid is part of a moat that runs through the park and is used as a waterway for the motor-propelled rubber rafts that take visitors on ridiculous "safaris."

Chicago's Lincoln Park Zoo has a spacious new sea lion exhibit. Most attractive and quite well designed for the animals, it does not incorporate a salt water filtration system. Their veterinarian, with whom we spoke, has "never felt the need" for such provision, indicating gross misunderstanding of these animals. Life expectancy for marine mammals at this facility, as in other zoos using fresh water, would indicate that the sea lions do not share his views.

Of the zoos included in our tour, one was equipped with adequate salt water filtration. Although many of their animals were picked up from the beach in poor condition, the San Jose Zoo (since phased out) enjoyed an enviable record for marine mammals, returning many to the sea after recovery.

Most others displayed seal pools which were dirty, full of algae and trash. In Philadelphia the usual flotsam of popcorn and marshmallows was supplemented by a few lead pencils. No effort was made by the staff to remove this material and thus avoid damage to the animals.

Californian sea lions in Brownsville, Texas, occupy a large pool of what appears to be pea soup. Excessive algae growth is accelerated by additional organic fertilizer from the monkeys and two river otters that live on the "island" intended for haul-out space. All the sea lions showed signs of photophobia on a shady day in April 1975.

The Marine Mammal Act of 1972, which temporarily

prohibits the collection of marine mammals, may improve the captive seal's lot, if not curtail its further capture. In any event, zoo directors would do well to solicit advice from those who fully understand marine mammals, and act promptly should they wish the few remaining seals and sea lions in captivity to survive.

4

THE CAPTIVE BIRTH AND BABY ZOO

A zoo birth, especially of an "endangered" and consequently "valuable" species, is cause for celebration in the administration office. Short of distributing the traditional cigar, the director happily accepts the role of proud father and graciously acknowledges congratulations from other zoos.

The predictable consequence of a boredom-provoked coupling is a bonanza for the zoo director, the institution, and makers of food for the parent animals. Literally everyone gets on the bandwagon. A photograph in the local newspaper accompanied by an absurd caption rounds out the event.

Parental joy may be short-lived. Many particularly sensitive species are nervous and irritated by the commotion brought about by what to them is a perfectly normal event. Exposure of a human mother to grinning, gesticulating apes who shine high intensity lights over her bed while others prod, measure, and photograph her newborn infant would be unthinkable. This is a normal experience for the female ape, tiger, or lion often aroused from cleaning or nursing her young on her cold concrete bed by a stream of curious visitors. Under these circumstances the animal may decide to leave her litter temporarily, possibly hoping that everyone will disappear.

Triumphantly, the zoo director pronounces the young "rejected by the mother." They are borne to a glass-fronted "nursery" to be raised by humans in an environment as remote from nature as that of their parents. White-coated attendants assume responsibility of the "abandoned" young and bottle feed them on schedule to the delight of visitors.

Some of the young will survive the artificial diet and Spartan ministrations of the well-meaning staff. The mother, fortunately, soon ceases to lactate and forgets her brief natural encounter, so everyone is satisfied. A "breeding success" is recorded, bringing favorable publicity to the zoo. Later the new animals will be sold to other zoos with inadequate facilities; their sale will bring cash for purchase of other specimens. The parents, meanwhile, unwittingly make preparations for a repeat performance.

It is not surprising that animals are born in captivity. Basic requirements are quite simple: two healthy animals of opposite gender in a situation that allows a meeting at the appropriate time. Births are quite commonplace in U.S. zoos, and if directors will give more thought to animal husbandry births will automatically become more so. It appears, from the number of surplus young of most species, that population control would currently be of primary concern.

No word holds more appeal to Americans than "baby." An adult elephant is impressive; a *baby* elephant elicits moans of ecstasy. Members of the general public, somewhat confused about the llama, are aware that it is either a high priest in Tibet or a Peruvian pack animal—depending on their literacy. Show them a *baby* llama and mass hysteria develops.

Understandably, astute animal dealers profit from this human frailty. Several magically named "baby zoos" operate in the United States. Some are permanent fixtures; others move from place to place like zoological gypsies. The young animals, generally purchased as surplus from larger zoos, are routinely prostituted to provide a photographic backdrop for grandparents and incidental exercise for the kiddies.

Unsupervised children do not understand that there is a limit to the handling an animal can take or the amount of garbage it may safely consume, and patrons of these facilities probably do not realize the discomfort these small creatures endure as they are "petted," pushed, ridden, or teased by children. At best, the baby zoo animal can expect indigestion and a few bruised ribs; at worst, an autopsy (if the specimen is valuable enough to warrant it) perhaps followed by a niche in the local Natural History Museum.

Ron's Children's Zoo of Riverside, California, combines business acumen with exploitation of wild animals. The owner, a member of the AAZPA, which enables him to purchase surplus zoo animals as well as "prohibited" species, graciously invited us to take pictures.

Mountain lions, wolves, and coyotes shared the squalor of dark, dirty five- by five- by six-foot cages. Four wooden sides with three-quarter-inch mesh covering the front admitted air but virtually prohibited passage of light. Pigeon parts, which the animals are fed, littered the floor, and the animals were a picture of despondency. Underneath the house, in mid-winter, several American alligators (protected by Federal law) were stored. A baby elephant, formerly available for petting, was a favorite until drug-oriented visitors fed the animal an overdose of barbiturate which quietly ended its show career. (Experimental euthanasia is not uncommon in zoos.)

An adequate indication of the apathy on the part of local humane agencies, this "zoo" also illustrates the incompetence of the USDA veterinary inspector who issues licenses to such primitive operations and the need for closer scrutiny by the AAZPA of member zoos' premises if they are to continue to represent American zoos.

Jett's Petting Zoo, which travels extensively in California, displayed an infant Asiatic elephant in San Jose's air conditioned Eastridge Mall shopping center. The little beast's respiration became labored, and a call was placed to the local zoo, which offered facilities for rest in an appropriate temperature as part of therapy. The petting zoo operator, anxious to keep prior commitments in Sacramento the following day, decided that the animal must make the trip—with predictable results.

Oakland's privately owned baby zoo has contributed substantially to animal casualties, including baby ostriches that attempted to appease early-morning hunger by eating filling but unnutritional goat manure. This recycling led to a prompt demise from malnutrition.

Pygmy hippos, left in the sun by inexperienced employees in this zoo, died from heat prostration. In spite of their appearance, they are not indestructible. These animals bring dividends to their owners by their permanent resemblance to baby hippos and are often bottle fed long after weaning to amuse patrons.

Porpoises, leased from a Miami dealer, were short-lived in their small pool, built to promote public feeding of the animals without consideration of bacterial transfer from grubby hands, until the owners decided to use hardier animals. A disturbing exploitation of California sea lions, instead, became part of the show. Feeding and petting these feisty little marine mammals is encouraged. A simple solution against potential lawsuits over bites has been incorporated into the exhibit: all the animals' teeth have been removed! (Seal lions, in fact, do not masticate food and can swallow quite large fish. This hardly justifies mutilation for promotion of food sales.)

A baby elk died from intestinal stoppage after eating wood shavings used as bedding for the nursing animal. In another facility belonging to the same owners, its mother could have raised the infant had it not been removed for the children's fun.

Ducks and chickens are literally chased to death, and pygmy goats (popular in petting zoos for their boundless capacity for food pellets dispensed at an enormous profit) lie bloated in the sun. They are given regular "rest" periods to recover in Oakland's baby zoo.

Baby chimpanzees, still cheapest of the apes and easiest to acquire, are exhibited in anthropomorphic surroundings in almost every petting zoo. Generally displayed in gaudy-colored pens filled with all kinds of toys, there is no doubt that the youngsters would be immeasurably better off with their parents. Monkeys chained or leashed to small platforms, owls and hawks tethered to perches, and birds kept in undersized cages for the amusement of small visitors are standard petting zoo "equipment."

Small visitors in Happy Hollow—for its animals a most inappropriate name—used a pointed fence post to perform exploratory surgery on a large desert tortoise which, of course, expired painfully some time later. On another occasion, vandals thoughtfully stacked picnic tables against the perimeter fence to allow deer access to the busy thoroughfare on the other side.

Animals raised in petting zoos do not always remain "tame" and gentle. Months of mauling, teasing, and exposure to humans can change inherent characteristics of even the most patient creature. Sooner or later, petting zoo animals display unusually aggressive habits, often to persons physically resembling former tormentors.

Sea lions can be fed and petted by children. Bite hazard has been removed with all of the animals' teeth. (*Baby Zoo, Oakland, California*)

It is most important that young animals taken from parents are placed in the care of someone firm, gentle, and constant, and not raised by a foster parent who "loves" animals and consequently spoils them, indirectly making their adult lives intolerable.

The trauma inflicted on petting zoo animals is to some extent associated with ignorance rather than sadism. Unqualified and underpaid help contribute to this situation. A security guard from Happy Hollow sought help from neighboring zoo personnel for a "horse with a prolapsed rectum hanging over its testicles." An investigation of this unusual event revealed a pony, in a corral with donkeys and heifers, stepping on a partly expelled placenta hanging to the icy asphalt floor. Reluctantly sent to a veterinary by San Jose Parks and Recreation Department supervisors, the pony was delivered of its foal. Until that time, nobody was aware that it was pregnant—or, apparently, of the animal's gender.

Most individuals operating "petting" or "contact" zoos are shrewd businesspersons who exploit emotions present in all humans, and are quite unqualified to operate their businesses. Strict supervision and guidance is imperative if loss of animal life is to be avoided. Stock should be restricted to domestic animals, which are by nature more durable, if no way to officially phase out these modern torture chambers can be found.

Enterprising persons taking advantage of human weakness will always abound. Gerald Iles briefly mentions, in his 1960 book, *A Home in the Zoo*, animal dealers in the U.S. He cites, unfortunately without identification, a letter from one who writes: ". . . the entire purchase for the kiddiepark was $250, consisting of rabbits, peafowl, mice and *assorted junk*."[30]

Charles Chase, a Miami animal dealer, imports tiny elephants which are often sold to "petting zoos." One of these little animals (thirty-six inches high) was "on inventory" in March 1974. The infant creature was in a wooden paddock, where it showed its need for companionship by frantic greeting with a diminutive trunk. The

Infant chimpanzee in typical "nursery" presentation, behind glass. (*Baby Zoo, Oakland, California*)

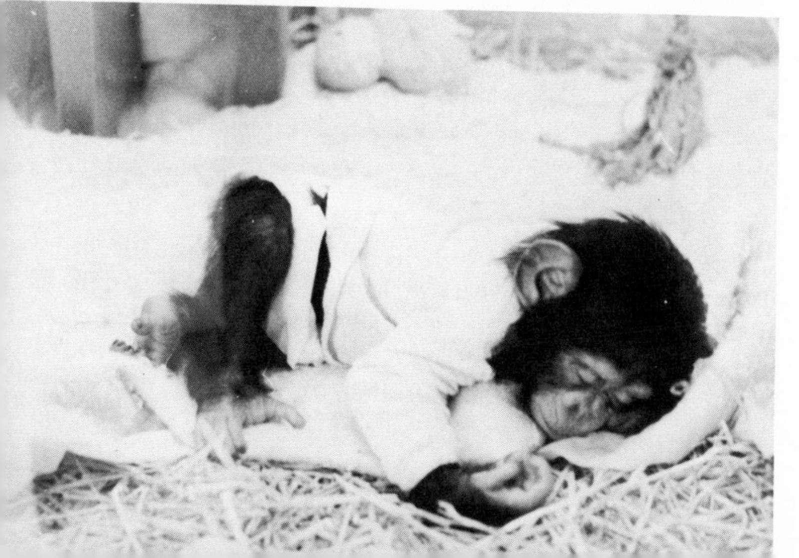

Baby chimpanzee in "animal care center" expresses feelings to photographer. (*Toledo, Ohio*)

stench of urine and manure in the holding warehouse forced us back to the office, where we learned that another, even smaller, was due in a few days and would be available for sale to the first comer. Baby elephants need care only a mother can give, and importation of such lone infants should not be permitted. Zoos and animal dealers who supply this demand for baby animals are to blame for the inhumane petting zoos, and action should be taken to curtail their activities.

It may be desirable for children to see wild animals at reasonably close range, and contact with certain species can be provided under capable supervision. Perhaps some day parents and teachers will recognize the distinction between playmate and plaything. One thing is certain—children will never learn from baby zoos.

Infant leopards removed from parent to provide window dressing for nursery. (*Colorado Springs, Colorado*)

5
NATIVE ANIMALS

Americans have developed a tendency to evalute by extrinsic rather than intrinsic worth. The most conspicuous spot in an art museum is usually occupied by a painting worth a great deal of money; the showcase of the jeweler centered by an expensive, large gem. They share a reverence for alien celebrities: adoration of visiting musicians, actors, artists or royalty suggests a belief that birth outside the U.S. guarantees superiority in intellect or talent, which is debatable. Natives, equally interesting, often have greater difficulty in finding recognition. It is not surprising that zoos follow this trend.

"Exotic," when applied to animals, is generally accepted as meaning "from outside" or "imported." Webster defines "exotic" as "strangely beautiful." Tigers, pandas, or Argus pheasants might be described in this way. Even their most avid enthusiasts have to agree that the hippopotamus and the warthog are short on beauty, however strange they may look.

Why Americans should find animals from other countries more appealing than their own is as hard to explain as why our zoos invariably treat native animals as second-class citizens. It is unlikely that TV audiences will ever watch Marlin Perkins in an exciting documentary featuring his removal of coyotes to a safe place as wilderness fires "encroach on their territory." Imagine his stalwart crew "tagging" pronghorn antelope or groundhogs for the benefit of their health!

Few spectacles are more engaging than a North American raccoon "washing" its food, with its head held back, lending the animal a singularly uninvolved expression. A family of native skunks on their nocturnal forage through suburban trashcans might qualify a close second. Scores of native animals are equally delightful to watch, whether at play, in search of food, or just mooching around. The late Walt Disney astutely capitalized on our wildlife in many of his productions. Zoo public relations persons seem to have overlooked this opportunity.

The National Zoo in Washington, D.C., operated by the Federal government, received a pair of giant pandas as a gift from China. Giant pandas are rare in their native Szechuan Province; to the National Zoo they are a priceless and prestigious attraction. In the new and quite pleasing panda exhibit, architects have shown exuberance creating a pseudo-oriental treatment in keeping with its glamorous tenants. Inside quarters are unashamedly contemporary high-priced condominium living rooms; outside, the paddock is turfed, with bamboo, shade, and a pool for the animals in case they decide to cohabit.

A short distance from this elegance, native hawks and eagles do not fare as well, and the twentieth-century ghetto dominates cage design. All over America, easily replaced indigenous animals are treated in the same cavalier manner. Wolves, coyotes, bears, badgers, and other natives live in concrete-floored pens of a size associated with the dog pound, where comfort is not of primary consideration, and occupancy mercifully brief.

Native birds, especially, are kept under unnecessarily Spartan conditions. The number of bald and golden eagles in undersized cages, often without screening or overhead shelter, is surpassed only by sea lions in dirty, fresh-water pools. We notice the eagles, which can apparently take a great deal of abuse, more because they remain alive and on display. (Sea lions have succumbed by dozens for years in zoos, but this was not common knowledge until visitors noticed an increasing number of empty pools.)

In other zoos, birds, especially raptors, have no shield from wind or snow. No concern is shown for these specimens during the long winter, which often lasts six months. Placed in open space with one perch, they sit and freeze in inclement weather.

Contrary to popular belief, these animals are no less susceptible to extremes of cold and heat than others. It does not seem to occur to zoo operators that choice of exposure or shelter is always available naturally; so their captive raptors' cages remain barren. Two buzzards in Bridgeport, Connecticut, sat on a lone perch thoughtlessly placed immediately under a rain gutter, soaked literally to the skin on a wet, cold day in February. Birds will invariably roost on the highest sheltered position that pecking order allows. It requires only fundamental good sense to incorporate some shelter over and around it.

Hawks and owls, natural enemies, are often placed together in cages. In Pueblo, Colorado, and Fresno, California, owls share small quarters with hawks. Needless psychological stress is placed on both species as a result of this arrangement.

In cages that restrict movement other than limited walking, and exposed on all sides to visitors, raptors are fed everything from dog meal to carrion. Overgrown talons caused by poorly made roosts add to their discomfort; broken and damaged plumage from attempts at flight in confined space are commonplace. A few major zoos have quite adequate hawk and owl exhibits, but most are much too small.

Some zoos "display" (if this term might be employed) eagles, hawks, and other raptors tethered to low perches, where they sit looking utterly bewildered, their legs entangled in the tethers. These primitive exhibits often include prominent signs publicizing the zoos' efforts to "rehabilitate" the unfortunate birds. In thankfully few zoos, the birds are "taught" to hunt by volunteers. Whether bird or human profits from the therapy is not made clear.

Alabama's Montgomery Zoo displays owls in small cages with a wire mesh floor which makes walking difficult. Birds with long talons become enmeshed in the wire and can damage tendons or break legs trying to get loose.

Native raptors are displayed in Phoenix, Arizona, behind glass without sanctuary. Birds cannot see the transparent glass and often fly wildly into it. Trauma could be eliminated by application of paper or paint to the window in the same manner that store owners protect humans from walking through plate glass doors.

In Moline, Illinois, golden eagles with wings amputated, presumably after injury, are kept in an adequate prefabricated cage. Unfortunately, the single perch is placed some distance from the ground and the one-winged birds have difficulty getting up to it. Their discomfort is compounded by omission of a security rail. This allows visitors to touch the birds on their high perch.

Jackson, Mississippi, displays four large eagles in a cage ten feet square. Midland, Texas, has a similar number in an almost identical roofless cage completely exposed to the bitter winter wind, and the sun in summer. Syracuse, New York; Fort Worth, Texas; Topeka, Kansas; and Carlsbad, New Mexico, display eagles in unsheltered cages, although some are of an adequate size.

Tulsa, Oklahoma, displays hawks in adequate-sized cages with stone shelters built on the floor, quite unsuited to these birds. (If these are intended as tornado shelters, we apologize.) Far away, the Buffalo, New York, zoo has an identical misconception of raptors' sleeping requirements.

In Terry Lou Acres, New Jersey, a display houses a four-foot American alligator. On a decorative rock in one corner of the small exhibit is a young American barn owl. Flight in the confined space is impossible. An attempt to fly would stop at the exhibit front, inevitably ending in the water directly below, to become a meal for the alligator. Perhaps the bird is actually part of the menu.

In the Como Zoo's "storage" cellar, pelicans are kept with sea lions in a small cage and pool which is monopolized by the large marine mammals and places needless stress on the pelicans. Small cylindrical cages used for screech owls and sparrow hawks in Boise, Idaho, and Tulsa, Oklahoma, are unbiological, and allow the inmates no flying space or privacy. Birds must never be displayed in cages where visitors can surround them.

A lone, lame roadrunner in a barren glass-fronted display in Cincinnati's zoo paced continually in front of the glass, tripping over rocks apparently placed there as window dressing.

A new exhibit in Columbus, Ohio, allowing considerable flight space, consists of a geometrical monstrosity designed, according to an informative sign, "especially for eagles." More familiar with angles than eagles, the designer provided only three-inch steel pipe and angle iron for roosting alternates—quite unsuited to the talons of these large birds.

There are a few large and suitable flight cages in zoos: Monroe, Louisiana; Cincinnati, Ohio; and Baton Rouge, Louisiana, have adequate displays.

American mammals get their share of the zoos' disdain for the non-exotic. Mountain lions, bobcats, cacomistles, raccoons, skunks, opossums, red and grey foxes, coyotes, wolves, otters, beavers, brown and grizzly bears, deer, pronghorn antelope, elk, moose, and buffalo are commonly used to fill run-down cages in our zoos.

Where exotic crocodiles are displayed, American alligators sometimes enjoy the comparative luxury of a warm reptile house. More often they are shown in muddy pools, often frozen over in winter. In a reptile farm in Hot Springs, Arkansas, alligators (truly endangered by Man's predations) are displayed, with typical irreverence for the indigenous animal, under explanatory signs which read: "This size alligator best suited for the making of purses, billfolds, and shoes." Other signs in the "farm" divulge some classic misinformation, including: "Alligators in this pen are from 200–250 years of age."

Typical examples of indigenous animal exhibits in zoos include Alabama's five bobcats displayed in a chrome and glass meatcase doubling as a cage, and seven raccoons in a crowded Little Rock pen with a concrete floor. An albino raccoon mating with a normal specimen in Fresno will undoubtedly produce freak offspring similar to an animal (from a previous litter) in neighboring Folsum Zoo.

In Syracuse, New York, coyotes and wolves were in open pens without shelter or screening of any description. At that time, twelve inches of snow covered the ground. Bridgeport, Connecticut, and Pawtucket, Rhode Island, displayed coyotes, raccoons, and a lone mountain lion standing in six inches of water during a winter sleet storm. None had dry quarters for retiring, and no attendant could be found for comment. Wolves and coyotes are housed permanently in dog runs in Lodi and Merced, California, and in several mid-West zoos. Lynx and foxes are in similar facilities in the "forgotten" section of Pittsburgh's zoo, a short walk from imposing buildings for "new" animals. Rochester, New York, displayed wolves in filthy snow-covered pens. Mountain lions, too, are housed in substandard displays, often overcrowded, almost everywhere.

Bald eagle, U.S. national emblem, in unsheltered cage. (*Rochester, New York*)

Salt Lake City exhibited strictly nocturnal cacomistles (ringtailed cats) in a brightly lit glass-fronted display without a hiding place. In an adjoining exhibit, a nocturnal cat lay as close as possible to a small rock in its display to avoid the bright light.

Larger animals are not much better off. A moose with glaucoma sloshed around its waterlogged pen in Como Zoo; buffalo in Attleboro moved thoughtfully through deep mud. The only dry large indigenous animals seen on our trip were buffalo, moose, and caribou mounted securely on the walls of the Springfield, Massachusetts, and Rochester, New York, zoos' indoor animal houses.

Native animals, in the right hands, can provide wonderful displays. Charleston Landing, North Carolina, has without doubt the finest exhibit for native cats in the country. An excellent and unembellished natural outdoor display presents mountain lions and bobcats in truly authentic surroundings, as close to nature as possible.

Bobcats are confined only by wire mesh guards tied to limbs of large trees, and the animals may be seen relaxing with feet hanging loosely over the large boughs under leafy shade. Mountain lions enjoy a similar existence.

Charleston Landing shows consideration for all its native animals—brown bears and alligators share a large area with a pleasant stream running through it. The park is a refreshing treat for discerning animal enthusiasts. We watched, with considerable regret, several casual visitors pass through the walk-through aviary without realizing that egrets and herons were perched high above them in the trees.

Boise, Idaho, is unique for its well-kept directorless zoo. Exhibiting mainly indigenous animals, their grottos for beaver, porcupine, and badgers supply everything the active little beasts could desire. The badgers, especially, are most intriguing as they burrow and reappear from the shambles of the display's earth floor. (A minor criticism might be aimed at the rather low safety wall on the visitor's side. It is

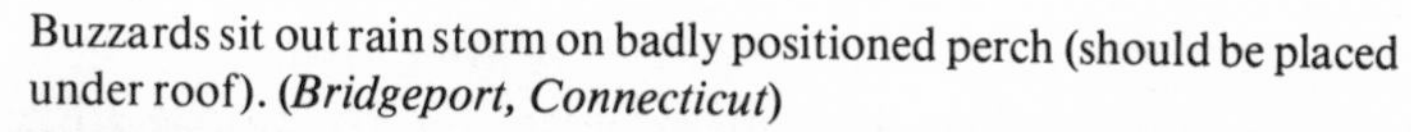

Buzzards sit out rain storm on badly positioned perch (should be placed under roof). (*Bridgeport, Connecticut*)

Injured eagles in cage without security rail. Visitors can surround cage and frighten one-winged birds. (*Moline, Illinois*)

easy to touch the animals by leaning over, and this could result in an impromptu manicure for an unwary visitor.)

American animals should enjoy at least equal status in housing and care to that of their foreign cousins, regardless of comparative market values.

Beavers are seldom displayed in zoos, although they are active, attractive animals when in a suitable exhibit. In Winston, Oregon, prior to the appointment of John Fairfield (who has since been replaced by yet another director), Wildlife Safari carnivores (endangered species) were fed beaver carcasses supplied by the local Fish and Game Department. This unique recycling of native animals to further conservation of the tiger and other exotic species can be attributed to efforts of the lumber industry in Oregon, which has contrived to have the beaver placed on a bounty. They are routinely trapped by state employees to prevent damage to valuable trees.

Zoo seals and sea lions (reviewed in greater detail in Chapter 3) are given prominence in zoos equal to that of exotic animals purely on the basis of their unusually buoyant characteristics. To recapitulate, with the exception

Owls in metal-roofed cage in desert heat. Exhibit is too open to visitors. (*Phoenix, Arizona*)

Fungus infected sea lions monopolize small storage quarters reluctantly shared by pelicans. (*St. Paul, Minnesota*)

Coyote huddles in rain storm—floor drains into den, leaving animal without dry refuge. (*Bridgeport, Connecticut*)

Cacomistles (ringtailed cats) hide from bright light in glass-fronted display. Nocturnal in habit, these animals need a dark shelter. (*Salt Lake City, Utah*)

of those in the better marine facilities, zoo marine mammals live notably short lives in uniformly squalid conditions. Regardless of the exhibits' decor, the same dirty fresh water is provided for swimming.

Most depend on handout feeding by the public and, invariably, aggressive or "smart" animals get the lion's share. Food in zoos is at best mediocre and at worst, a substance made from ingredients which have the texture of sandpaper-covered polyethylene, which only very hungry animals will eat.

Eye problems are routine. Many sea lions are blind or will be if they survive long enough. There are more zoos with poor seal facilities than otherwise, and some new ones built at considerable expense are no better biologically than the oldest, algae-covered, spiked-fence exhibits.

Supervisor puts sick seal through routine for synthetic food reward. Animal is suffering from acute photophobia and is undernourished (note protruding vertebrae). (*San Antonio, Texas*)

Familiar sight on the Lone Star State side roads. Coyote, hung on fence post as "warning to other coyotes" by Texan rancher.

Most pathetic of all the miserably housed, cold and wet, silently suffering native zoo animals was a sea lion in the San Antonio, Texas, zoo. The "supervisor of mammals" put this emaciated female Californian sea lion through an excruciatingly sad series of "tricks" which incorporated a walk, sideways, across a metal rod supported by two trestles. The animal was thin, one eye was closed and the other reduced to a slit from photophobia, and its vertebrae and ribs showed prominently through its half-dry fur.

As a reward for its performance, the animal was thrown, from time to time, a piece of synthetic food from a filthy tin can tied to the supervisor's belt. The animal was in need of therapy, a diet of suitable fish to restore its weight, and salt water in its pool. Possibly the few lay persons who watched the "show" noticed nothing amiss. For us it was unforgettable—and totally unnecessary.

The moratorium on collecting marine mammals has deprived zoos of new animals, and half of their seal pools are empty. At last count (1974), more than 600 marine mammals were on order from dealers to replace losses over the previous eighteen months.

Indigenous animals receive ill treatment from other sources. The many coyotes seen hamstrung, gutted, and hung on fence posts along highways do little to promote the image of big, friendly Texans. Not unnaturally, ranchers wish to destroy predators caught in the act of killing cattle. The dead animals we saw were on land incapable of supporting anything larger than rats, much less livestock. Scores of squashed raccoons, opossums, and squirrels on the road provided diverting conversation during most of the trip; to them, death at least came more quickly.

The Humane Society of the United States (HSUS), which supports humane treatment of our wildlife, stated in a recent pamphlet that sodium fluoreacetate (known as "compound 1080") used by the Department of Interior against coyotes killed 90,000 coyotes during one year. This poison is tasteless, odorless, and colorless. There is no antidote, and it is not biodegradable. The HSUS points out that along with the "target" animals, 21,000 bobcats, 2,800 red wolves, 24,000 foxes, 800 bears, 300 mountain lions, 1,200 beavers, 7,000 badgers, 19,000 skunks, 7,600 opossums, and 6,700 porcupines also died.[31] These appalling figures show the contempt in which our wildlife is held by the U.S. government, and the ease with which industry bulldozes legislation permitting this indiscriminate slaughter.

Whether or not our zoo directors (also dependent for their livelihood on public funds) share the Department of Interior's views on American animals is unknown. To preach conservation of foreign animals by placing them on "vanishing species" or "endangered" lists while the native animal is so poorly treated, both as a captive and in its wild state, is blatant hypocrisy.

6
EXHIBIT DESIGN

A keen competitive spirit is evident between zoos in exhibit design, notably among the larger—and from their viewpoint, better—facilities. Selection of the least practical and biological display would present a problem if an award were to be presented.

Almost total accord is reached in respect to external design features in a uniform vulgarity. It is obvious that a large percentage of public funds earmarked for improvements to zoo animals' living quarters is applied to facade. Money left over for the animals' actual living conditions is often insufficient, and they are invariably the ultimate losers.

Conversely, this uniformity is not apparent in good design features seen only in the few facilities fortunate enough to have competent and forceful direction.

Observed in most zoos were slippery or inappropriate floors; dangerous projections; insufficient light and floor space; bright-colored paint and/or dirty water in marine mammal pools (eye irritants); absence of security fences or rails, climbing or exercise facilities, retiring space, and heating or cooling; improper installation of wire mesh;

unwise use of glass for certain animals; dangerous restraint methods; and countless other faults.

Design faults and omissions cited in this chapter pertain to the larger zoos whose directors should be qualified to recognize and correct them. Shoddily built, untenable structures used for animal display throughout the country in less prestigious facilities are too numerous for individual comment, so we must show charity in assuming that their administrators are unaware of the defects and do not have the expertise to rectify them.

(*1*) *Window Dressing*

People prefer to see animals in what they think are "natural" surroundings, and do not recognize the faults in design. "Open" and "natural habitat" exhibits are built for this reason rather than with consideration for the animals' comfort.

Quite often the synthetic habitat offers the inhabitants less than a well-built cage exhibit. One of the dreadfully drab cages in the Philadelphia Zoo's primate house has been livened up by addition of a fiberglass jungle scene. A sign to the effect that "it will be interesting to see the animal's reaction to its new habitat" may by this time be gross understatement. Embellishments of this nature are purely for the benefit of the zoo visitor, although the animal may find temporary therapy in dismantling the man-made habitat.

Amusing innovations were in progress at the Erie, Pennsylvania, zoo in February 1974. An overpowering odor of acetone pervaded the primate house where gorillas and chimpanzees pass solitary lives in tiled cubicles approximately twelve feet square—tastefully furnished with a raised tile dais where the animal presumably sleeps and something like a card table anchored to a heavy chain, the

Workman making fiberglass jungle for visitors; gorilla will be viewed in its tiled cell through artificial trees. (*Erie, Pennsylvania*)

function of which could not be determined. Two employees were fabricating quite elaborate fiberglass trees, complete with leaves, in front of the ape displays. When finished, visitors will be able to enjoy an instant safari by looking through the branches (which are on their side of the moated exhibit) to see the animals in their cells.

Sonora Desert Museum's beautifully detailed landscape scenes are definitely pleasing to the human eye, but fiberglass and other materials of this kind are no more biologically suited to the animals in the displays than concrete-floored cages. Aesthetics are of secondary importance to the captive creatures: Sonora's mortality is no less alarming than in any zoo.

"Open" and "habitat" displays that allow concealment at will are psychologically sound for captive animals, but have little advantage over a barred cage if this sanctuary is not incorporated into the design. Cages with free access to shelter give a sense of security to an animal by permitting voluntary isolation or proximity to visitors. Knowledge of this alternative permits the occupants to relax at the front of a display, often with arms or paws through the bars. Where no sanctuary is available, animals stay as far away as possible, with their backs to the visitor. Large cats and primates are especially prone to behave in this way.

(2) *Artificial Climates*

Many zoo deaths are attributable to cold and damp, which affects tropical animals to the greatest extent. Heating in many zoos is non-existent—outside the administrative offices. Many directors believe that their animals should be kept in local climatic conditions without artificial assistance.

In zoos where needless sacrifice of animals to weather conditions is not routine, attempts to keep animals warm are often misguided. Electric infra-red heat lamps are frequently used, especially in aviaries. The low cost of the lamps (about $3) and ease of installation and replacement are probably primary reasons for their use. Unfortunately, they have disadvantages that may not appear important to the designer. Heat generated by the filament is reflected to a focal point about four feet from the lamp. The spot of heat produces severe infra-red burns on anything within this range. Birds roosting by these lamps are often burned in an attempt to get closer to the heat source. Although lamp instructions clearly mention this hazard, few zoo people seem to have read the warning.

The Children's Zoo in Los Angeles houses two-fingered sloths from South America. These animals need an enclosed display with properly controlled heat, but are exhibited on a shelf in a wire mesh-backed cage, huddled below a heat lamp attached to the outside of the mesh. There is no doubt that they will be slowly toasted, as sloths have a high pain threshold and pay little attention to discomfort until it becomes intense. By this time the damage will be done. (Los

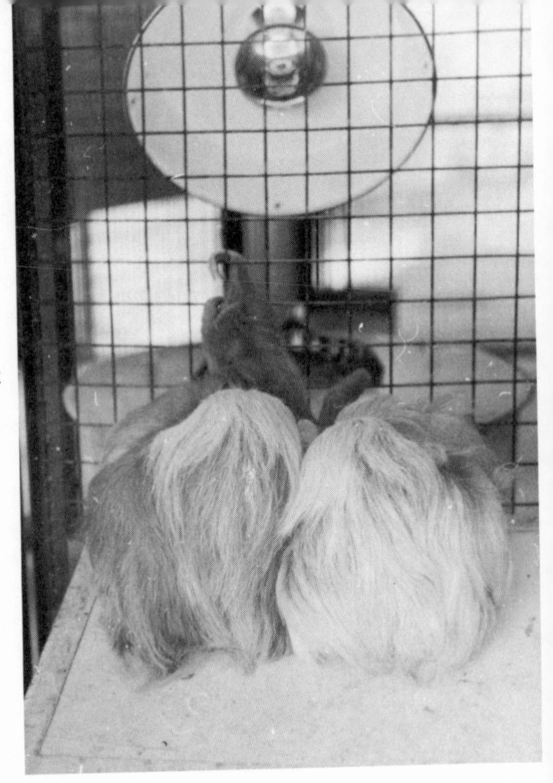

Two sloths on unnatural flat surface exposed to burns from infra-red lamp. Heated air, not focused heat lamp, should be used to warm animals. (*Los Angeles, California*)

Angeles Zoo employees, better organized than the sloths, fare better—snack bars and souvenir kiosks are glassed in and well heated.)

Several very efficient infra-red heaters particularly suited to use in indoor or outdoor animal exhibits are marketed. The effort involved in locating suppliers seems to be the barrier to their use.

In zoos where heating is insufficient or unavailable, shelters must be designed to preserve body heat. Metal oil drums, which double as animals' sleeping quarters and nesting boxes, are hardly ideal.

Small cages scattered through Phoenix, Arizona's, zoo for birds and small mammals are topped with corrugated metal roofs. With Phoenix's temperature extremes, occupants are faced with the ordeal of being barbequed in summer and frozen in winter.

An alternate "shelter" seen frequently in major zoos consists of a length of large-diameter concrete sewer pipe. This of course, is little better than an oil drum.

Perhaps directors who prefer these forms of shelter flunked their basic physics courses, so are unaware that body heat must be conserved if an animal is to be comfortable, or that uninsulated sheet metal is not generally considered first choice for heat retention.

(3) *Antiques*

Many basic exhibits in American zoos are reminiscent of the early European bear pits. In these antique displays, visitors looked down on the backs of the captive animals. Reluctance to change characterizes the zoo hierarchy, and designers continue to build these pits.

In Birmingham, Alabama, large cats are displayed almost twenty feet below eye level in concrete pens which become intolerably hot in summer. Zoo bear exhibits embody this antique design feature, and consist basically of an uncolored concrete area of variable size sloping toward a twenty-foot drop into a dry moat. Few have provision for unassisted egress if an animal should fall or be pushed over. In such emergencies, a crane is used, bringing further trauma to the already distressed animal.

The Bronx, New York, zoo is an exception. A huge natural rock provides the backdrop for the finest bear exhibit in the country. With a few foxes, the Kodiaks share pools and climbing and exercise space unequaled in U.S. zoos. This exhibit is part of Bronx's somewhat pedantic but progressive staff's effort to improve the archaic zoo.

An interesting modernized "antique" in the San Diego Zoo shows that designers grossly overestimate visitors' physical capabilities. A series of repetitious buff-colored concrete corrals, appropriately dubbed the "Hoof and

Horn Mesa," house hoofed animals which bear boring similarity to their immediate neighbors. Visitor response was so negative that an overhead ride, common in ski resorts, was built at a cost of several million dollars to avoid a total write-off.

The ski lift traverses the zoo, and for a dollar and a half, the footweary visitor may view, from fifty feet above, the backs of the hoofed and horned stock with a bonus of cage tops thrown in. Unlike the original exhibit, the ride is popular and brings in about a million dollars a year.

(*4*) *Errors and Hazards*

Hilly terrain in the National Zoo makes an attractive setting for hoofed stock. High weeds have been left undisturbed for the browsing animals. Loosely stacked, heavy rocks are used in terracing the exhibit. Standing near the edge of the shelf formed by the rocks, animals may slip and damage tendons and hooves when the soft earth causes the rocks to collapse—two individuals in a herd of rare Père David's deer were lame.

Trees in the exhibit are protected from foraging animals by a ring of jagged rocks. The potential hazard to the valuable animals, conspicuously labeled "endangered," should eliminate use of this dangerous means of tree preservation.

Their elephant house—which, incidentally, contains other large animals—boasts power-operated sliding doors in the exhibits. These labor-saving devices are useful, but without occasional maintenance, which may be unavailable at the zoo, they can become death traps.

In August 1974, a baby pygmy hippopotamus was badly mauled when a sluggish door mechanism failed to close in time to prevent the infant from straying into an adjoining paddock. An unsociable adult neighbor promptly bit several chunks out of the infant animal. Fortunately, an alert keeper witnessed the malfunction and saved the baby from more serious injury.

Oakland, California's, joint sun bear, reptile, and tiger exhibit is an exemplary combination of ignorance of the animals' requirements and contempt for public safety.

Two young Bengal tigers were purchased and placed in the exhibit, which originally featured an unsightly array of vertical bamboo poles attached to the small floor—presumably the designer's attempt to achieve a "pop art" jungle effect. Quickly destroyed by the animals, the concrete anchors remain to further detract from the appearance of the exhibit.

The tigers used the moat, which occupies most of the exhibit space, for swimming. They quickly learned to jump to the roof and potential freedom in the park. On one occasion, a lady visitor drove one of the youngsters back into the display with a blow from her umbrella.

Discreetly disposed of, the tigers were replaced by less acrobatic African lions. These animals still occupy the exhibit, and spend the day waiting for the door to their sleeping quarters to open.

A reptile exhibit, wedged between tigers and bears and viewed from the back of the complex, showed similar negligence in planning. The minimal heat generated by a few infra-red lamps quickly dissipated through superfluous vents in the roof, and many reptiles died until a keeper with more than a passing interest in herpetology came to work at the zoo. He rectified the situation by plugging the vents and installing suitable heaters.

The newer synthetic African veldt display is more pleasing to the visitor's eye although its animal losses have been fairly high. It provides sharp contrast to nearby cages of a design generally associated with traveling circuses.

Most captive elephants live in poorly designed exhibits, with dangerous and poorly executed methods of restraint.

Elephant restraint is dangerous; animal has wound on side corresponding to spikes welded to rail. Spikes should be removed. (*Little Rock, Arkansas*)

The Little Rock, Arkansas, zoo displayed elephants with untreated wounds coinciding with spikes welded to the inner edge of restraining rails. Injuries of this nature could easily be avoided by a logical modification—removal of the spikes from the exhibit.

A design error which should be corrected in Boise, Idaho's, zoo, has placed the restraining mesh in front of one display, at an angle. The narrow shelf installed halfway up the mesh for the monkeys' recreation is mounted too closely, and fur on the animals' sides has been removed by friction during movement along the shelf. Repositioning would restore the monkeys' fur and add greatly to the appearance and comfort of the animals.

Vertical, cylindrical metal cages for sparrow hawks and small owls in the same zoo have five-inch-long metal rods welded to the central supporting pipe for roosts. The limited space in the cage makes reaching the perches difficult for the diminutive birds.

Anteaters are on display in a sunken exhibit in Kansas City, Missouri, as inappropriate as its concrete floor. On the other side of a raised walkway, hippopotamus are obliged to execute complicated maneuvers (for a hippo) through a narrow channel to reach their haul-out area.

A fairly new giraffe house with an outside corral where the animals are confined by a walled, dry moat could be considered one of Baltimore Zoo's more innovational displays. Decorative facade in the form of pseudo-African war shields provides an unusual hazard. Placed about two feet apart with their lower edge approximately half the height of an adult giraffe, the shields are attached to the building in a manner which allows the animals to put head and neck between the back of the shields and the glass window of the indoor exhibit. Sudden panic could result in broken glass, lacerated animals, and general pandemonium among the giraffes and their ostrich corralmates, not to mention any visitors inside the exhibit.

Friction from wire mesh keeps these monkeys furless on both sides of body. Shelf should be moved to prevent animals' contact with wire during exercise. (*Boise, Idaho*)

The moat, presumably designed to display the animals' heads at eye level, has a roughly circular concrete retaining wall to hold back the soil. Giraffes and ostriches nonchalantly step down to walk in the moat and look over the visitor security rail. Zoo patrons standing near the entrance may be confronted with a huge head and neck hanging three or four feet over the rail. During our visit, people were stroking the giraffes' heads (quite potent defense weapons), while ostriches pecked at their toes through the lower portions of the rail. Architectural extrusions in the moat are further safety hazards in case of stampedes during social disputes.

Water barriers can be attractive and safe if they are carefully engineered with thorough knowledge of the animals to be confined by the moat. Zoos all over the world have learned through sad experiences that water-filled moats must be planned to suit individual species' requirements and physical abilities.

A large number of primates, carnivores, and hoofed stock have been lost by drowning in panic situations. The Gladys Porter Zoo, in Brownsville, Texas, originally featured, almost exclusively, deep moats filled by the ubiquitious green-brown resaca (overflow) waters of the Rio Grande. Keepers and a zoo board member helplessly watched a frightened female lion, transferred from a traveling cage, drown after futile efforts to escape from the unfamilar exhibit.

This episode may change the designer's apparent belief that all animals are inherently able to swim; many species cannot, and those that are able to navigate under normal conditions are quite often drowned in panic situations.

No water-moated exhibit should be built without safety features for animals that unintentionally fall into the water. These should be visible and suitable for prospective occupants. Philadelphia Zoo's tiger exhibit has a deep moat. A simple emergency escape for the tigers, which are generally quite at home in the water, consists of a section of chain link fence attached to the front of the exhibit and reaching into the water. This sensible addition is hardly noticeable to visitors, but speaks well for the person who installed it.

Apes, which do not naturally swim, must never be housed in water-moated displays unless adequate measures to restrain them from entering the moat are incorporated. Shallow pools should be provided in the exhibit for bathing and play.

A spacious gibbon island, isolated by a knee-high water moat, had not opened in Kansas City's zoo at the time of our visit, but should provide interesting animal-visitor contact when the agile apes become familiar with their shallow wading pool.

The Topeka, Kansas, zoo carries togetherness a little too far in an exhibit where visitors, with little effort, may hold hands with a fair-sized American alligator. A gibbon ape in an adjoining pen increases probability of this encounter by grabbing unsuspecting humans as they pass.

(5) *Plagiarism*

Originality is not the average zoo director's forte, and zoo exhibits throughout the country show shameless plagiarism. Perhaps it is easier to take a surreptitious peek at an exhibit built by a neighbor and try to make one just like it from memory. In doing this, even the exhibit's faults are faithfully copied.

Perhaps the outstanding example, including potentially fatal restraint methods, may be seen in Cleveland's spacious display for skittish, small antelope and deer, animals notoriously unpredictable under stress.

A concrete ditch, approximately two feet deep and five wide, isolates animals in this exhibit from visitors. For some

Rhinoceros's horns completely worn away by nervous head swaying in pen with badly designed restraint. Lateral bars would be preferable. Animal needs rubbing post in pen. (*Washington, D.C.*)

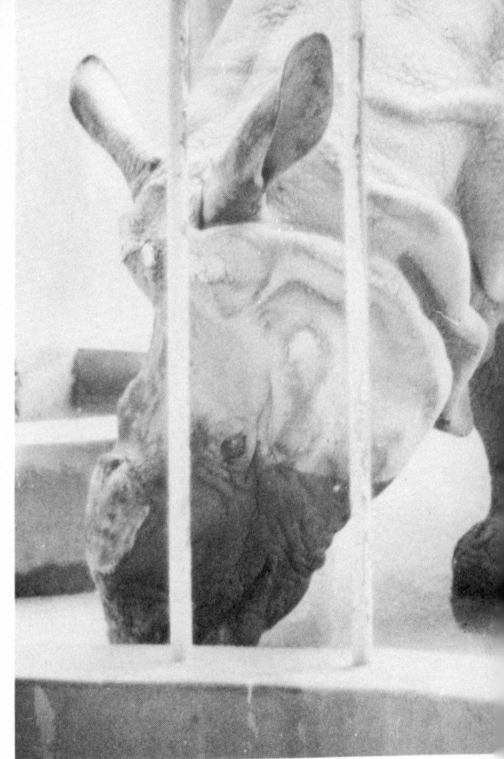

Spikes on inside of Kodiak bear cage present hazard to animal; no extrusions are permissible on interior of animal enclosures. (*Baltimore, Maryland*)

Ornamental "war shields" attached to wall of giraffe display hazardous to animals and public inside exhibit. Panic could result in broken plate glass and injury. (*Baltimore, Maryland*)

Visitor contact of this nature is dangerous. Security rail is too low; alligator is small but capable of inflicting painful bite. (*Topeka, Kansas*)

Pronghorn antelope with permanent disfigurement as a result of injury from collision with restraint under panic situation—not infrequent with these shy animals. (*Boston, Massachusetts*)

five feet on the animals' side of the display, foot-high jagged rocks cover the ground, constituting an unnecessary hazard. Complementing this unbiological arrangement, the ditch is covered with a metal grille with bars approximately five inches apart. Damage to livestock attempting a panic crossing of this animal trap can be imagined, especially when taking into consideration the animals' natural tendency to run blindly from trouble, real or imagined.

An identical exhibit in neighboring Toledo suggests a sharing of bad ideas: the original designer is not to be complimented for his ingenuity. Finding a similar exhibit in faraway Memphis, Tennessee, was an unpleasant shock. Their African veldt display, however, includes a sign indicating less than total confidence in the arrangement:

> Several species of MAMMALS and BIRDS frequently found living together harmoniously in the wild state can be observed here. *Due to the nature of this exhibit, the numbers and kinds of animals on display will change frequently.* (Emphasis mine)

Arizona's Sonora Desert Museum is a well-presented and -maintained facility where only animals indigenous to the desert of Arizona are displayed. Attention has been paid to details in the "habitats," and even the everpresent simulated rocks are hard to detect.

Installation of a small chain-link "penthouse" on the roof of the mountain lion exhibit is an unusually thoughtful feature. This inexpensive, and not unattractive, addition gives its occupants a panoramic view of the desert by climbing a ramp.

In underground exhibits which form the rear of outside displays, visitors may press a button and look through one-way glass at sleeping raccoons or groundhogs, in a dim light, without disturbing the animals.

A designer in search of ideas apparently failed to take careful notes for later use in New Mexico's Carlsbad Botanical and Zoological Gardens, and omitted important details for the underground dens resembling Sonora's. The

Restraint for hoofed stock would be catastrophic to inmates in panic conditions. Reaction would be to jump over jagged rocks into metal grille installed over concrete ditch; injuries to long legs would be severe. (*Toledo, Ohio*)

Carlsbad visitor, on pressing a button, sees not a sleeping animal but a startled beast rudely awakened by the bright light that illuminates the den and a large area of the dark viewing tunnel.

(6) *Extravagance*

Designers in Phoenix, Arizona, may have consulted with ghosts of the ancient Druids on their modern gorilla display. The magnificent animals could look no more out of place in Stonehenge, where there is at least some grass between the huge pillars. The blistering Phoenix sun must keep the immense off-white structure hot throughout the summer. Their simple open lion and tiger exhibits with turf floors are much more biological and attractive.

The primate house, recently built in Kansas City's zoo, has a majestic and entirely superfluous glass-sided, tapered roof. Inside the impressive structure, winter quarters are typical ape cells with perhaps slightly lighter and shinier steel restraining bars. Not a masterpiece of zoo design, this

Gorilla exhibit: costly, unbiological, architectural monument unsuited to any animal, especially in extreme heat encountered in desert area. (*Phoenix, Arizona*)

Facade: upper section of building is superfluous and serves no useful purpose. Inside ape quarters are little better than the old cages used in most zoos. Money should be used for animals' comfort. (*Kansas City, Missouri*)

exhibit was probably appreciated more by the construction company awarded the building contract than by its occupants.

Toledo's zoo boasts glass-sided kiosks with unbiological, smooth floors for long-legged birds of assorted species. The surrealistic appearance of these tall creatures as they walk carefully on the shiny floor adds to the visual confusion of open concrete exhibits, which permit partial see-through viewing of adjoining displays throughout the zoo.

Concrete security walls for visitors are low and potentially dangerous. Adventurous patrons have found their way into exhibits on more than one occasion, according to the security guard who obligingly opened the exit gate. (All zookeepers had left the zoo right on time, leaving visitors inside.)

The Knowland Park Zoo, in Oakland, California, is situated in a fairly large and hilly park overlooking the unattractive city and suburbs. An eye-catching metal tower dwarfs the entrance and its cartoon animal motif.

Glass windows and smooth concrete floors are better suited to hardware display. Long-legged birds occupying these extraordinary cages need firm footing, roosting facilities, and screening. They should never be exhibited in see-through museum displays. (*Toledo, Ohio*)

Resembling an airport control tower mounted on a long pipe, this monstrosity was intended to display gibbon apes in mid-air. Topped by a fiberglass umbrella, chain link mesh hangs untidily over steel cables anchored to a concrete base that forms the floor and doubles as a hazardous landing pad for simians losing their grip on the metal trapezes.

Sleeping quarters at the top of the tower are accessible only by way of a tunnel connecting with the base of the pipe. An unfortunate duty keeper (usually a junior employee) climbs this each day to service the animals' heated sleeping quarters.

A spiral ramp leads visitors to a viewpoint about halfway to the top of the cage to give an effect that could have been accomplished in an exhibit half the height, without the expense of building a ramp. Externally impressive, the structure provides an incongruous setting for the apes.

Initial casualties among the gibbons were so frequent that the skill of Dr. Ray Young, former director, couldn't keep enough gibbons on display, and spider monkeys were substituted. The extra hold provided by the monkey's prehensile tail has given them a much longer life expectancy than their predecessors.

Topeka's plastic-domed rain forest was not yet open to the public in March 1974, but we were allowed to inspect it. A first impression of noisy fans and a thundering waterfall, issuing incongruously from a rock wall near the center of the building, still remains. The rain forest's designer's concept of housing for lesser jungle mammals is poorly manifested in the unusually small concrete-walled pens intended for them. The complex "temperature and humidity control center," which (according to Assistant Director John Wortman) will require a full-time human operator, combines traditional large-scale thinking and the effect of bureaucratic delays that whittle away at funds.

The walk-through aviary in Stoneham, Massachusetts, is a huge glass building reminiscent of the old dirigible maintenance hangars which still mar the countryside on Air Force bases. This expensive structure devotes too much space to walkways and platforms. Planting is minimal, and deficient ventilation creates an unpleasant musty odor. Colored panels placed at random over sections of the glass cover lend a cathedral-like atmosphere to the exhibit and distract from the birds on display.

(7) *Gingerbread*

The Turtleback Zoo in New Jersey is a mixture of sublime and ridiculous. A pink fiberglass pig contains an Australian kookaburra (a large kingfisher known as the laughing jackass) that peeks nervously through small glass portholes in the pig's sides.

Sea lions adroitly avoid the corners of a small dumbell-shaped swimming pool that restricts movement and has hazardous extrusions. It is spanned by a small bridge.

Whimsical theme: fiberglass pig houses Australian kookaburra. It is totally inadequate for any animal, and belongs in a childrens' playground. (*Turtleback, Newark, New Jersey*)

Emus, antelope, and zebra are exhibited on a hazardous rocky ground surface totally unsuited to these animals. Delightful little houses in the exhibit do not fit the requirements of the long-legged beasts.

In Jackson, Mississippi, a minature coastal village—complete with nondenominational church—is part of the otherwise standard zoo monkey island. Walls restraining this enlightened group are of economical concrete but have been laboriously hand painted to simulate natural rock. The effect, to be truthful, is not all that might be desired.

Bird shelters (admittedly an unusual feature in our zoos) have been made in the form of small houses, replete with painted windows and drapes.

The new Los Angeles Zoo is outstanding for facade, bewildering route signing, and terrain which would confound a Sherpa guide. Built on a hill which must deprive most of California's well-fed citizens from enjoying it, a battery of aviaries is exposed to weather extremes and the

Floor surface for zebra dangerous; rocks do not permit captive animals to move safely in their pen. Zoo staff should clear entire area of obstacles before working on further playground equipment. (*Turtleback, Newark, New Jersey*)

Anthropomorphism: village, complete with non-sectarian house of worship, in monkey island gives no advantage to jungle animals. Labor wasted on decorations might be used to advantage elsewhere. (*Jackson, Mississippi*)

city's famous smog. An exhausting tour of the entire zoo dulled our curiosity as to the purpose of the expensive twin-pagoda-roofed building which dominates the zoo.

The main entrance is equally extravagant and inappropriate, and the walk through the beflagged mall into the zoo portend what a visitor may expect inside.

The Dutch motif chosen for the entrance of Indianapolis's zoo includes a full-scale windmill and Dutch cottages which are complete with a worried-looking fiberglass European stork standing in a plastic nest on an artificial chimney.

The elephant exhibit, a miniature Taj Mahal, houses an African species which, when we visited, was enthusiastically eating aluminum foil as a chaser for popcorn supplied by a kind visitor.

(*8*) *Collectors*

Many directors are avid collectors who find pleasure in the accumulation of zoo animals. Overcrowded zoos exemplify their success. Reduction of animal inventory is to them synonymous with loss of personal prestige.

In St. Paul, Minnesota, the Como Zoo—like flying saucers—must be seen to be believed. Nowhere, in any country, may such a singular assortment of captive animals be observed in such bizarre living conditions under one roof. Fortunately for the general public, the unspeakable cellar "winter quarters" are off limits. A new geodesic dome, built traditionally well below eye level, houses some young gorillas who will soon be stronger than their "modern" home.

What the Como Zoo has to offer even vandals is a mystery, but a security guard's April 1974 report reads in part: "Drunk Indian inside zoo throwing snowballs at animals. He disappeared before I could get police." (The remainder of the report deals with intimate ethnic detail and is omitted.)

A visit to the Como Zoo is a unique and surprising experience discerning zoogoers should avoid.

Situated over the snack bar in Baltimore's zoo, the second-story indoor bird house cunningly blends the charm of the Natural History Museum with Rod Serling's *Twilight Zone*. In what appear to be discarded London telephone booths birds are displayed behind glass in dim light to maximum disadvantage. Our visit culminated in ejection from a springloaded door opening outward over thirteen precipitous, rickety steps. Not until completing a tour of the remainder of the zoo was it apparent that this is the star exhibit.

Only a few directors have reached the sensible conclusion that without funds there can be no new or improved exhibits, and they are making use of a logical alternative: reduction of stock to a manageable number by humane disposal of some animals. Removal of partitions between existing small cages provides more space for fewer inmates.

There are pitifully few zoos—mostly small ones—where directors show common sense and concern for their animals by building comparatively inexpensive, biologically sound displays satisfying to inmate and visitor.

Among these is the misleadingly named Child's Estate Zoo in Santa Barbara, California. Far from being a children's playground, this neatly arranged facility is an example of what can be done with sensible use of limited funds. Many of its occupants were born in the zoo, and all have lived several years under Assistant Director Susan Black's ministrations.

Director Ted McToldridge, who has been with the zoo since its original beginning in 1963, is a versatile man who likes building things and knows how to do so. An excellent capybara exhibit, including all that the animals need, is tribute to his design capabilities; well-placed lion and tiger displays complement the animals. Sound routine policies and an unusual willingness to work make this zoo a refreshing change from the multi-million-dollar architectural catastrophes found in our larger zoos.

Salisbury, Maryland's, director also shows that a lot may be done with little money. The clean, attractive zoo has well-planned displays, mostly on grass. An excellent jaguar display is surrounded by shrubs on three sides—a most unusual concession in favor of the animal. Only the security rail might be considered slightly inadequate, but an alert staff apparently has had no problems there.

Orangutans and gorillas at the Gladys Porter Zoo are displayed on excellent, turfed outdoor exhibits suited to the benign Gulf climate of Brownsville, Texas. Overenthusiastic use of pneumatically applied concrete, which lent a cake-frosting appearance to the new zoo, is being relieved by the addition of wooden displays, including a spacious and airy walk-through aviary. Biological requirements and aesthetics are being given greater consideration in new exhibits than in the original design, to advantage.

The Bronx, New York, zoo has built a fine indoor display for birds. The World of Birds has been designed with care and thought for inmates as much as visitors. Although the equipment is somewhat noisy, the general effect is excellent.

Other affluent zoos have followed New York's lead and a few such specialized exhibits are to be found. Denver's new tropical bird house promises to be worthy of Director Freiheit's interest and expertise with birds. He showed us the exhibit in the last stages of construction, enabling us to see the innovations for preservation of prospective inmates. In most zoos, the director's penchant for a particular form of animal life is manifested in these new buildings.

In the remaining majority of our zoos, design defects are numerous. While it is not always possible to achieve perfection, an attempt to rectify faults in existing exhibits and the use of more common sense in designing new ones is reasonable to expect but seldom forthcoming.

A sign near the entrance of Muscatine, Iowa's, pathetic menagerie reads:

"HELP US BUILD A BETTER ZOO."

Its appeal is appropriate to a large percentage of America's zoos.

7

VANDALISM AND MORTALITY

It is doubtful whether any American zoo has escaped vandalism in some form by sadistic, ignorant, or dimwitted humans. Incidents have not been widely publicized and are often suppressed by public relations-minded administrators. Nevertheless, zoo animals are maimed, mutilated, and killed quite frequently.

Some vandals operate during visiting hours in zoos short on security. Others, generally more vicious, satisfy their strange urges after the zoo is closed.

Theft of zoo animals is less common and can involve "inside" assistance, especially when a large or boisterous specimen is involved. A trio of would-be animal dealers stole a young tiger from the San Francisco Zoo, unnoticed by the security guard. It was later located after a dealer reported an attempted transaction involving the cub. Returned eventually to the zoo, its death a few weeks later was attributed to improper diet during its "capture" and exposure to domestic animals.

Educated vandals fulfilling fraternity initiation requirements stole a spider monkey from the monkey island at the same zoo, adding to its long list of vandalism.

Security is lax in other city-operated zoos. Oakland, California, has repeatedly been the target of vandals. On one occasion, reptiles, including large snakes, were stolen from a closed exhibit, which must have taken considerable time. Another visit to the zoo by vandals left alligators with their eyes gouged out and several birds with broken legs from thrown rocks.

San Pascual Wild Animal Park has a considerable number of trained security guards, but not enough to prevent a cheetah cub from being removed by unauthorized persons. Rare pygmy marmosets were also stolen from the San Diego Zoo by individuals who seemingly have an insight on market values in the pet trade.

Vandals do not respect barriers designed to protect visitors and animals. A drunken San Francisco man vaulted over security rails and a moat into the lions' exhibit and was mauled (not badly enough) by a male animal that was shot and killed by a society board member who happened to be around. The incident was newsworthy and widely pub-

Zoo sign indicates mentality of clientele in Folsom Zoo. Patrons who need this kind of advice could replace the animals here. (*Folsom, California*)

licized: coverage generally portrayed the skid-row citizen as a hero for his "narrow escape" from the lion.

The Como Zoo lost a polar bear, shot on the director's orders, when an inebriated youth attempted to make friends by jumping in its moated exhibit. A polar bear in the badly designed Springfield, Massachusetts, exhibit (with no security rail) was shot when it grabbed a man who had persistently teased it. A revolver bullet, fired by a policeman into the bear's eye, distracted the animal and remains lodged in its skull. The bear, still on exhibit, has fits of screaming from pain caused by the bullet's pressure.

New York City's zoos, currently objects of considerable discussion by hordes of "experts," are familiar with vandals. Recently, fallow deer in a pen were beaten and a pregnant doe killed by youths who climbed a high corral fence. A polar bear was shot and killed by police when it seized the arm of a teasing visitor.

Numerous zoo animals have died by ingestion of articles offered or thrown by visitors. Symptoms displayed in such cases are often misleading and tend to delay appropriate treatment until it is too late. It is not unusual or a sign of impending disaster for a zoo animal to refuse or only partially finish a meal; like humans, they sometimes like to be quiet and isolated from penmates. Consequently, most foreign bodies are generally recovered at autopsy.

Hippopotamus have been the target of such vandals for years. Many have died from injuries caused by swallowing Coke bottles, sticks, and other debris. Visitors seem to believe that tennis balls are a suitable diet for zoo hippos.

Giraffes in Birmingham, Alabama, were poisoned by visitors, according to keepers. A fine male Alaskan fur seal raised from infancy in the San Jose Zoo suffered perforated intestine a few days after swallowing a small metal screwdriver thrown into its pool.

Californian sea lions have been killed by swallowing

foreign objects in Garden City Zoo, Kansas. Other sea lions there were stoned to death. The zoo boasts no security, is open until 11:00 P.M., and permits car parking in front of exhibits. A most unusual polar bear display in the same facility houses the mate of an animal that escaped and was shot when a keeper ran into difficulties in returning it to the cage. A baseball field, also in the zoo grounds, is rather unique.

Zoo inhabitants have been maimed with sticks, rocks, and an assortment of handy weapons wielded by unbalanced or inebriated patrons. They are by no means a rarity. A visitor to San Jose, California, threw sand from the marine mammal exhibit into the eyes of a sub-adult elephant seal, salvaged from the beach and recuperating in the zoo, causing acute discomfort. Reprimanded by zoo staff, the man, who was accompanied by three young children, indignantly replied: "Well, there's no sign saying you shouldn't"—a statement which prohibited an immediate or courteous response.

Youths threw explosive fireworks, known locally as cherry bombs, in San Francisco's sea lion pool, stunning all and blinding one animal.

Veterinarians called to treat zoo animals hurt by vandals could supply countless details. Only incidents resulting in human injury are required by law to be reported—for public health reasons. As no similar legislation applies in respect to injured animals, the majority of incidents are quietly forgotten.

An indication that zoo directors may be slowly becoming aware that vandalism must be halted, or recognize it (at least among themselves) as a major problem, is a February 1975 article in AAZPA's monthly bulletin. Under the heading "Stolen Animal Survey" it solicits information from any zoo that suffered *loss of stock by thieves.*[32] The article, quite appropriately, originates from the impregnable San Diego Zoo. Perhaps this will spread eventually to concern for vandalism involving *injuries and deaths* to animals as well.

Zoo publications and administrators tend to minimize animal abuse by visitors. The director of the Indianapolis Zoo told us, during a visit, that there had been no recent cases of vandalism. Five minutes later a keeper revised this with "not much recently—except for a giraffe stabbed with a pitchfork by a visitor!"

Zoos polled in 1974 in connection with research for this book either keep few records of vandalism or take it as part of routine, and show a marked reluctance to provide reliable data. Answers to our questionnaire with respect to vandalism and mortality varied from "minimal" to "none." Publicity which points a finger at administration deficiency is avoided like a plague by most directors.

Vandals are by no means responsible for all of our zoo mortality. Inadequate husbandry may be blamed for many losses. Other deaths are caused by exhibit design incorporating hazards to animals—especially those with long legs and nervous dispositions. Many have drowned in water-filled barriers, and more from trauma resulting from falls into dry moats. The same pattern may occur several times before the mistakes causing the accidents are rectified.

Several giraffes in Los Angeles's zoo panicked or were pushed to death in their badly planned exhibit. An Associated Press release mentions that a "team of specialists" who later inspected the zoo found no base for charges of animal mistreatment, but "believed the zoo was underfunded and had been poorly designed in some respects." (The understatement of the year!) The team of specialists comprised directors of the San Diego, Colorado Springs, and Topeka zoos, all fellow AAZPA members. The team (what an appropriate word) reached "no conclusion as to whether slippery cage floors had contributed to the deaths of the giraffes."

L.A. zookeepers, more discriminating and less tactful, filed a fifty-page report challenging the inspection and called the team's favorable report a "whitewash."[33] (Keepers are often more concerned over their animals than some zoo directors, who hesitate to criticize even an incompetent peer—at least openly.)

Further evidence in support of the keepers' views appears in an unexpected source—*Playgirl* magazine. An article on Dr. Rosalie Reed, veterinary for the Los Angeles Zoo, mentions that she has done everything (with animals) in the zoo, including "performing a necropsy on a giraffe that had lost its footing on the slippery floor of its enclosure and died of trauma."[34]

Poor judgment by staff members who try to mix incompatible species in a small display has killed hundreds. At Safari World, California, introduction of a female tigress to a lone male tiger quickly ended with a bite on the neck. The female died almost immediately. This male had previously killed an African lion in a similar manner. A Cape buffalo at Safari World greeted a keeper one morning with an elk impaled on its formidable horns. A llama was killed in the same display.

In World Wildlife Safari, Winston, Oregon, unwise staff members caused another tiger's death but gave a psychologist a lifelong opportunity to make some classic statements. He is quoted by United Action for Animals from notes taken during a speech made at a meeting of the American Association for the Advancement of Science.

> The resident male killed the newly introduced male very fast. Uninhibited aggression. Now I think these kinds of studies done in wild animal parks give me pretty fair deductions about social organization in wild tigers.

He might also learn why vanishing species continue to vanish in our zoos. He went on to say that he would like to see a study on reactions by aggressive zebra to other animals introduced to their territory in wildlife parks, and ended with, "It should be a damn fine study."[35] For whom?

An attempt by the director to reconstruct a piece of African veldt in San Francisco Zoo resulted in killing of an ostrich and a zebra by a territory-conscious wildebeest. Further "habitat" trials there included a mixed display of black bears and Arctic foxes: the bears ate the fox kits. Coyote pups served as snacks for grizzly bears in another "experiment."

Wild animals surviving capture often die during their first few days in zoos. Special consideration should be extended to new arrivals; often a quiet shady spot will do wonders for an animal in unfamiliar surroundings. It is not unusual, though, for an animal to be abruptly evicted from a traveling crate into a permanent exhibit. Directors who permit this show ignorance of the captive animal and indifference to its comfort in their immature desire to "show off" their acquisition.

Mortality has been so high in captive marine mammals that almost half of the zoos in the country had dry pools in 1974. El Paso, Texas, has changed its seal pool to an alligator pool. They may fare better than the sea lions; one died abruptly from a broken neck while being restrained by staff.

Tortoises in Warner Bros. Jungle Habitat died of pneumonia in unheated pens during the winter. Their number ranges from an admitted fifteen to an alleged twenty. Evansville, Indiana, lost 60 percent of their birds from a cooling system in a new building designed so that they were exposed to a continuous draft.

Fresno Zoo, California, lost a pair of black rhinoceroses in six months: the first from effects of cold and the other from an accident at night unnoticed by security guards. A giraffe was found dead one morning in Abilene, Texas, from a broken neck. There was no security guard on duty.

San Antonio Zoo's clouded leopard's mate adorns the director's office wall. Skins of a leopard and tiger share this distinction. Skins from fifteen animals, ranging from wolf to leopard, that died in the zoo graced the "answer men's" table in St. Paul, Minnesota, to allow visitors a "total experience."

No attempt is made to enumerate the routine loss of animals in zoos by what, if zoo directors were licensed professionals, could only be described as malpractice. The number of wild animals killed during capture, or that die in zoos through human error and incompetence only to be

Rare clouded leopard "conversation piece" on director's office wall. Animal's mate is still alive on display. Good taste prohibits use of the zoo's failures as wall ornaments. (*San Antonio, Texas*)

Skins of animals from zoo make interesting contrast to remaining live animals housed in building, but do not indicate good husbandry. (*St. Paul, Minnesota*)

replaced by animal dealers whose agents contribute to further losses, runs into many thousands yearly. Deaths by vandalism are to no less degree the responsibility of zoo administrators.

Zoo directors currently do not account to any government agency for animal deaths. If they did, mortality statistics would indisputedly point a finger at the neglect and ignorance of persons who are, in the majority, paid by our taxes. We share guilt by allowing this to continue.

Different criteria are used in compiling animal mortality. Directors are conscious of the appalling loss of stock and use any means of keeping statistics to a pleasingly low number. Many zoos do not include deaths in livestock less than three months on display. The true figure, obviously, is the number of specimens that die at any time after entering the zoo for display.

There are a few zoos whose losses are high but whose directors or veterinaries feel that they should publicize accurate figures. Some quotes from their reports follow. Reference to these zoos, or to data they have compiled for publication, is accompanied by commendation for their honesty. Acknowledgment of accidental and sometimes needless deaths shows courage and professionalism. With these statistics, perhaps other zoos will learn from their experience, and possibly take steps to prevent losses from similar causes.

The unforgettable New Orleans Zoo, mentioned previously in respect to its director's abhorrence of artificial heat, lost in 1973 a male sable antelope, a bison, two rhesus monkeys, one coatimundi, and two Californian sea lions from lung-associated diseases. With the exception of the sea lions, the deaths can be attributed to damp, cold quarters. Indicative of an unobservant staff is an entry which reads ("Mammal Deaths 1973"): "American otter—too decomposed for necropsy."[36] Did nobody notice the animal's absence from daily feedings and find it before it decomposed?

Cheyenne Mountain Zoo's (Colorado) 1969 report cites the deaths of an orangutan from "pneumonitis," a spectacled langur (leaf monkey), pronghorn antelope, three llamas, African leopard, wombat, binturong, gibbon ape, sable antelope, and douc langur (leaf monkey) from pneumonia and associated lung problems. Losses in this prestigious zoo for reasons listed as "undetermined" included a binturong, American bison, gemsbok (antelope), Bengal tiger, Himalayan tahr, and an American elk. Deaths due to injuries (which incriminate unobservant keepers) included one eland, one binturong, one white elk, a llama, one black and white colobus monkey, one dromedary (camel), one white-tailed gnu, and one European red deer. Twenty monkeys died in the New World Primate Research project. Quite an impressive total. Comparative statistics in the yearly report (the latest we could find) showed that 1969's deaths were 2.5 percent greater than in 1962.[37]

Cheyenne Mountain quite correctly counts all animals from the day they enter their zoo in compiling statistics, which is unusually honest.

Buffalo, New York's, annual report for 1973 frankly states that some losses were due to food or foreign objects, and cites rubber bands, coins, and a baseball among them. It also recognizes fighting among animals as a cause of injury or death. Hoof trouble is mentioned as a problem, with the hiring of a "professional" hoof trimmer who comes to the zoo on a regular basis as a solution. Now that these problems are accepted as fact, perhaps Buffalo's director will start to control vandalism in an appropriate manner, train keepers to recognize incompatibility between exhibit-mates to avoid fighting, and do something about conditions (display floor or diet) which will reduce hoof problems.

Mammal, bird, and reptile losses in Buffalo were in line with most other zoos. Deaths classified "reasons undetermined" include one Reeves muntjac, an Patagonian cavy, one striped hyena, one opossum, one wallaroo, one Malabar squirrel, one Barbados sheep, an American porcupine, a tamandua, and one wallaby. Pneumonia accounted for one mouflon sheep, one Himalayan tahr, one African lion, a Karakul sheep, one gemsbok, and one otter. Among mammals euthanized (many directors prefer to see animals die lingering deaths rather than lose an exhibit) were a meercat, two Barbados sheep, a Tasmanian devil, a North American porcupine, an American elk, a nutria, and a striped hyena. Buffalo Zoo reportedly lost 56 out of 402 mammals, as well as numerous birds and reptiles in 1973.[38]

We emphasize that the zoos' veterinary reports show only losses. Often zoo veterinaries are not called until it is too late for successful treatment. Observant and well-trained staff can improve animals' chances for recovery by a prompt call for assistance.

PART THREE
THE FUTURE OF THE ZOO

8

IMPROVING ANIMAL CARE

References are made to only a few animals, but zoo living conditions for every species will be improved if priority is given to concern for animals, with convenience of zoo visitors and zoo staff relegated to second and third place.

(1) *Inspections*

A daily inspection of every animal by a qualified person, other than the animal's keeper, is an essential part of zoo routine. Zookeepers have daily contact with their charges, but this familiarity makes it easy to miss minor discrepancies while doing their work. It is essential that someone else check the entire zoo. Inspection must include every animal, every exhibit, and any equipment used in animal care.

In a medium-sized facility this can be accomplished in two hours—not a great deal of time when expense and trouble saved by daily observation by the right person is taken into consideration. Inspections should be made on foot—a quick tour through the facility on an electric cart is not enough. It is imperative that notes are taken by the inspector; zookeepers cannot be expected to remember all details noticed while working.

The procedure is almost unheard of in America. (Santa Barbara director Ted McToldridge is probably unique in helping clean the zoo.) Some directors are qualified to make a meaningful inspection but seem to be tied up with bureaucracy, and either too tired or lazy.

Keepers are responsible for seeing that discrepancies do not go unattended and reporting them daily to a supervisor. Animal reports from keepers should be verbal and written to avoid misunderstanding, and mandatory when physical problems need urgent attention. An alert keeper becomes frustrated when observations are habitually ignored by supervisors, and he may develop a tendency to omit mention of things which could be important. All keeper reports should be promptly investigated.

San Francisco trainee zookeeper Tom Huff noticed that a Malayan tapir was not eating and had difficulty moving. He told the head keeper, who replied that the animal often "acted strange" and to forget it. Huff filed a report, emphasizing his belief that the animal was seriously ill. The following morning the animal's condition was worse. Huff went again to the supervisor, who refused to look at the tapir, told Huff that he would be reported for insubordination if he didn't go back to work, and that if the animal died it was not Huff's concern.

The next day the tapir was unable to stand and was breathing with difficulty. Huff ran to the head keeper, crying, "The tapir is dying." The head keeper told him to wait, and went to the animal. In a few minutes he returned and said, "She's dead—get back to work." Huff resigned from the zoo after several similar experiences, and is currently an associate director of Stanford Institute for Herpetological Research.

(2) *Cleaning*

Professional zoo persons understand that cleaning is important to animal husbandry in the zoo, and that it must not be considered a menial task. Zoo cleaning should be done in the morning, preferably before the gates open to the public. (Most visitors do not find cage hosing, or unpleasant odors sometimes present during washdown, interesting.) For the keeper, cleaning is a splendid opportunity for checking animals' physical condition. Loose stools, blood or vomit, and other abnormalities are easily seen; keepers are given a chance to look for them and to greet the animal while they examine it at close quarters without being distracted by visitors.

During cleaning operations, animals should be checked for signs of estrus, stress, or incompatibility with penmates,

Sign in Baltimore's rundown zoo. Procrastination by city staff contributes to state of exhibit here. (*Baltimore, Maryland*)

which are sometimes more pronounced when humans are present. Lameness or stiffness, as animals move around in the morning after their night's rest, are easily noticed. In aviaries, feathers and other debris are an indication of trouble. Problems with birds tend to develop shortly after dawn, so early-morning aviary cleaning is preferable.

Care must be exercised in choice of chemical compounds for cleaning animal pens. Phenol, the base for most disinfectants, should not be used for felines, as toxic or fatal doses may result from contact or ingestion. For the fastidious, one pharmaceutical company manufactures a disinfectant cleaner that leaves a masking fragrance of gardenias.

Chlorine is a familiar and readily obtainable chemical. Despite an acrid odor, it is unexcelled as a safe, efficient bactericide and algae control. Zoos should use a dilute solution, powdered and granulated chlorine or liquid gas. Gas requires delicate equipment for safe distribution and considerable caution on the part of persons who use it, as inhalation can be fatal.

(3) *Meals*

Animal food must be prepared in absolutely clean facilities and handled as if it were for humans. Food preparation can be used to advantage as a display (except in zoos where the food is considered too bad for the public eye); people are interested in knowing what food is eaten by different animals.

Kitchen equipment should be complete and include freezer, large refrigerators, meat grinder, commercial blender, and accurate scales. A deep double sink with ample hot and cold water supply is essential, as well as a large sturdy table for cutting meat and other food. A wheeled dolly or gurney saves labor, and rubber tires make its progress through the zoo less irritating to visitors and animals. Stainless steel dishes are preferable and easy to clean.

Meat should be thawed gradually overnight and completely unfrozen before feeding. Portions should be cut just before serving to retain the maximum amount of juices. Fish must be thawed slowly, never in hot or warm water, and should be washed in running water until thoroughly clean prior to feeding.

Some directors permit keepers to throw fish into a seal pool containing several animals, depriving the less aggressive and slow eaters of a fair share. This can lead to malnutrition or starvation. Marine mammals need a measured amount fed by hand to suit size, species, and appetite. Vitamin/mineral supplements are beneficial to their good health. Capsules may be inserted into the gill cavity of an appropriate number of fish; these should be given before feeding the entire ration. (Animals that might not finish their normal quota are at least assured of their daily supplements or medication.)

This procedure works quite well for many birds and mammals. Supplements may be concealed in grapes, pieces of banana, and other fruit for birds that prefer to swallow food whole (hornbills, toucans, etc.). Carnivores readily take medication or supplements in small chunks of meat slotted to accommodate the capsules. Additives are preferably given before the main meal, as large cats will ignore small pieces if the entire ration is visible.

Where several birds of different sizes share one display, it may be prudent to use several bowls in compensation for pecking order difficulties. Fruit for birds should be peeled and cut to suitable size to ascertain that they are all able to eat the food. This eliminates leftovers—skins, pits, etc. —which attract flies and vermin.

Staff feeding zoo animals should be familiar with their eating habits and typical acceptance of food. Abnormal reaction to feeding can indicate pending sickness, and animals that show sudden changes in feeding patterns should be watched closely for other symptoms. Whenever possible, keepers should measure and prepare food for their own animals. Feeding is preferably performed by as few people as possible—ideally, the same person.

For convenience, a group of carnivores can be easily trained to eat together in the same exhibit. Cats quickly learn to remain in one section of the "territory" until their portion is fed. When this is done, it is advisable to feed single large chunks of meat rather than several small ones. Cagemates who finish eating first are apt to steal small scraps from the floor, which results in superficial wounds and strained relations. It is expedient to arrange feeding sequences so that the dominant animals get their food first, as they tend to leave their territory as soon as food appears.

Zoo animals obliged to eat substitutes for natural foods should be given special consideration. Great anteaters, tamanduas, pangolins, and most of the edentata can digest nothing larger than a minute particle of food. If too coarse in texture, loose stools and eventual serious rectal damage will follow.

The Waring Company manufactures a commercial blender of a gallon capacity that reduces literally anything (including finger tips) to a fluid consistency. Although these appliances are readily available in restaurant supply houses, they are used in few U.S. zoos. (Some marine mammal facilities employ them in preparation of formula for infants, as the blender converts whole fish to a creamy liquid in minutes. The liquid is warmed by friction during the process to a temperature suited to tube feeding baby animals.)

Parasite-free animals fed formula blended in this manner readily ingest their ration (which eliminates contamination by flying insects) and excrete stools comparable to that of their wild counterparts. (For coprophiles, wild anteater stool is black, pelleted, quite dry, and, not surprisingly, composed largely of partially digested ant and termite heads.)

(4) *Grooming*

Zoo animals are seldom washed, unless for a publicity picture, by rain, or by accidental hosing during cage cleaning. Many captive animals enjoy a bath and feel better for an occasional shampoo, weather permitting.

African lions are rather lethargic and will often lie in their urine to avoid moving to a dry spot. The male of the species is particularly inclined to laxity in this respect, so the shampoo practice is fine for them. Luxurious manes and fur on zoo lions are often dirty; washing untangles the unsightly and doubtless uncomfortable matted fur and eliminates its attendant nebula of flies.

(5) *Shelter and Heat*

Nature provides wild animals with suitable cover, sometimes under the earth or in ground cover and tall trees. Wild birds roost in heavy foliage, generally on outer branches where predators large enough to harm them hesitate to tread. Specialized birds such as the hornbill nest, lay eggs, and hatch young in holes in high trees, sealed in by their mates for several weeks. Room service is provided by the busy male, who collects food and brings it to the female; she is able to put part of her bill through a narrow slit left in the plaster. The ratites (ostrich, emu, cassowary, and rhea) are endowed with a flat breastbone and sleep on the ground. Truly nocturnal animals are seriously affected by direct light and become emotionally upset by excessive exposure. Very few zoos have adequate quarters for these specialized creatures, and their short lives in captivity are made miserable by needless stress from artificial or natural light.

A little consideration can increase comfort for zoo animals, all of which need shelter from rain, cold, sunshine, and wind.

All birds should have, and will readily enter, a small box or shelter appropriately placed in an exhibit. In addition to providing refuge and momentary freedom from stress, a shelter can simplify transfer of larger birds by its use as a transport cage.

Exhibits for every animal must include some sort of hiding place, though it may be used only occasionally. Surprisingly few zoos provide them, and if used they are often built in inappropriate places. Shelters for eagles and hawks are sometimes built on the ground—quite unsuited to most flying birds.

Ostriches and rheas customarily live in open spaces, but the cassowary is a furtive shy bird that prefers virgin forest. In captivity it appears more at ease when given a shelter. Most zoo cassowaries are housed at night in barns or sheds, which to them is little better than being in an open field. Shelters that are just large enough for the bird to turn around in and have a door approximately the height of the bird's back are ideal. Hay or straw should be provided for a bed. Cassowaries will spend hours inside shelters with their heads sticking through the door. Ratites should never be kept on smooth hard floors.

Shelter door openings facing away from the public allow maximum privacy. Wood is a suitable material for construction, and the shelter can be an attractive addition to a display. Visitors could learn that all animals do not like to spend the entire day in the open.

If boxes must be built on the floor, they should be a few inches higher than ground level to prevent flooding during heavy rain or cleaning. A sloping floor allows prompt drainage of any water tracked in by the occupant.

A den for large cats should be big enough for them to stretch out on its roof. This can be electrically heated to keep them warm and visible on the coldest days. Obviously, a waterproof roof must cover the den, and they must be screened from wind.

Reptiles generally live in temperatures of over 70 degrees. American alligators are no exception. In captivity their water should be kept at an appropriate temperature. Heating may be accomplished in several ways. An immersion heater, suitably shielded to prevent injury to the animals, is probably the cheapest method. One alternate method consists of an infra-red heater mounted a few feet high over the pool and part of the haul-out area. This gives an additional advantage by providing dry warmth if the animals prefer to be out of the water, but is more costly.

Birds may be heated safely by the latter method. Mounting the unit about twenty feet from their roost assures an even distribution of warmth over a considerable area. Wind does not affect infra-red heat transfer, so tropical birds can be maintained comfortably during the worst weather if overhead and side shelter is incorporated. Thermostatic controls are advisable with either installation to protect the animals against excessive heat and save expensive energy. Heat lamps should not be used other than for emergencies, as the principle of operation is different and even brief exposure to its focused heat can be dangerous.

Application of some common sense and a modicum of basic carpentry will alleviate needless discomfort from thoughtless design. Screening and access to sleeping quarters or suitable hiding places will promptly relieve stress on certain species that suffer from total exposure to sunlight or visitors. Animals that habitually burrow in the earth are less frustrated on an unbiological concrete floor when sanctuary in a dark box is available. In many instances, repositioning a perch will keep birds dry and sheltered from wind and rain.

Thatch can be applied to roof surfaces. It is waterproof, a good heat shield, and most attractive. It can be attached in a manner that prevents climbing animals from pulling it apart or eating it.

(6) *Help from Nature*

Landscaping plays an important part in the zoo, and strategically placed shrubs and shade trees of a nonpoisonous variety make the zoo more pleasant for the animals and attractive to visitors. Only nondeciduous trees should be used.

Almost all animals feel better on turf, which greatly enhances the appearance of any exhibit. Grass cannot be grown successfully in an exhibit while occupied by animals, but turf or sod is readily available and easy to install. After the instant lawn is in place, animals can be persuaded not to eat it by judicious application of steer manure every few days. Grass and trees need attention and nourishment, and it is illogical to expect them to thrive without water and fertilizer. They should be considered expendable and subject to replacement when disturbed by animals.

Ungulates kept on turf benefit from an apron of abrasive concrete laid inside their exhibit perimeter. Obliged to walk over its surface daily en route to water, food, and sleeping quarters, the concrete will help keep hooves normal.

A few animals, including sloths and binturongs, can be exhibited without restraint in a tree of suitable size during the day and placed in a warm shelter at night.

Selection of materials for use in zoos is critical. Small rocks, gravel, and wood chips become handy missiles for vandals and must be avoided.

(7) *Public Feeding*

Sunday morning hangovers are customary to a great many humans. Similar symptoms occur in the zoo on Mondays: more animals throw up, have diarrhea, and display symptoms of the previous day's overindulgence. This phenomena cannot be traced to anthropomorphic zookeepers trying to give the animals a night on the town. Sunday generally brings more people to the zoo, and more visitors throw the animals more peanuts, popcorn, marshmallows, cookies, and other indescribable garbage packaged for human consumption. The result of their "kindness" is found on the floor Monday morning—as well as occasional corpses of animals with bloated stomachs.

San Diego Zoo is crammed with food concessions and machines. Intended for visitors, much of it, with its non-biodegradable packaging, goes into animal exhibits despite token vigilance by staff.

San Antonio, Texas, has a veritable battery of food machines to dispense food for every conceivable animal. (It is more or less identical in shape, color, and odor.) Patrons can develop immense biceps pitching it to fat animals that condescend to eat only those morsels that fall within an inch of their mouths.

In zoos with seal pools, it is customary to see fish exposed to the sun in dirty buckets or kept under-refrigerated in less than spotless machines to be dispensed to sea lions by sweaty-handed children. Combined with dirty water lacking essential minerals, these animals become particularly vulnerable to stomach upsets from public feeding.

Public feeding is encouraged in commercially minded zoos, frowned upon in better facilities, and should be prohibited by law everywhere. It is as lethal as rock throwing, and although some humans find feeding en-

Without comment! (*Sacramento, California*)

Elephant stretches over spiked mesh for peanut. Exhibit incorporates double hazard: public feeding, and wrongly installed chain link fence. Wire should be installed with spikes on floor to prevent injury to animal. (*Sacramento, California*)

Youngster on wrong side of security rail feeding animals; adults are apparently unconcerned (this is typical of zoo visitor attitudes). (*Cincinnati, Ohio*)

tertaining and therapeutic, it kills hundreds of assorted species every year.

Public feeding can be discouraged by removal of all vending machines, snack bars, and other food sources from the zoo. While they remain it is impossible to remove the hazard and unrealistic to rely on public cooperation alone.

(8) *The Seal Pool*

In bona fide marine facilities, marine mammals thrive in clean salt water when fed regulated amounts of assorted varieties of high-quality fish and supplements. Permits to exhibit seals and sea lions should be issued only to zoos that provide similar conditions.

Where sea water may not be readily available, 100 pounds of marine salt diluted in 300 gallons of fresh water gives equivalent salinity, and trace minerals found in natural sea water may be added as diet supplements. Salt-resistant filtration of sea water involves Teflon-lined tanks and plastic plumbing, but is no more complicated than fresh-water treatment.

A handful of zoos have filtration systems, but most sea lion pools, including San Diego's, are simply large holes covered by concrete with provision for drainage. Water is dumped when it become opaque and is replaced by tap water, which often takes hours. These archaic systems may be found in almost all American zoos. Water saved in one year's operation would pay for a filtration system, which uses very little additional water once installed, but most directors do not seem aware of this.

There are several filters on the market; most manufactured for swimming pools and totally unsuitable for seal pools. Bathroom habits of marine mammals differ from those of normal humans, and a heavy-duty, high-capacity unit is required to remove wastes from seal water.

A system properly engineered for a given number of animals will provide crystal clear salt water assured of minimal loss of salt or water. In this medium marine mammals of all species may live long, active lives. There must, of course, be no public feeding.

(9) *Security*

A zoo without a fence places its animals in jeopardy. Security fences are imperative for a zoo regardless of its location. Basic zoo security starts with a fence at least eight feet high and topped by heavy-duty barbed wire.

During the day security consists primarily of curbing exuberant patrons with their offspring, and is better performed by zoo staff or volunteers patrolling the zoo grounds. Their vigilance can be of great assistance in controlling crowds, giving information as requested, and keeping visitors on walkways and out of exhibits and mischief. Their function is one of prevention and restraint rather than actual guard duty.

Animals must never be left unattended: security guards should be on the zoo premises from the time visitors leave until zoo staff return to work on the following day. There is little to be gained by improvement in husbandry for zoo animals if they are to be stoned, speared, or shot to death by vandals after closing hours.

Night guards principally carry out the duties of a police officer, but they can also be of assistance in the prevention of casualties to zoo inmates. They can be trained to recognize abnormalities in the animals at night. On their rounds, guards should be on the lookout for unusual activity among the inmates, a change of sleeping or roosting place, and restlessness or distress. They should check all heaters, lights, and animal-associated equipment for proper function.

Domestic animal in Como Zoo building; keepers and "educational" volunteers permit this unwise practice. (Disease transfer and stress on caged animals is not desirable.) (*St. Paul, Minnesota*)

Foxes await fingertip snack at unprotected cage front. Children should be supervised at all times while in the vicinity of wild animals. (*Moline, Illinois*)

Guards need not correct faults but must report them immediately to the director, who must take care of the problem. Night workers should be instructed to avoid shining lights on the animals—particularly birds, that may panic and fly blindly into obstacles. If a bird falls to the aviary floor at night, caution should be used to avoid frightening the remainder of the occupants while removing it.

The problem of blatant vandalism has faced every zoo—the majority of these without security staff. Night guards should be compulsory for zoos, and although the USDA can insist that "qualified personnel" are on duty at all times, it does not.

Closed-circuit television coupled with sound has been successfully used in some zoos to supervise daytime vandals. At night electronics can facilitate the security guards' task by warning of an illegal entry. Photo-electric equipment can help locate prowlers or electrically charge a perimeter fence.

Potential vandals have no morals and must be summarily dealt with. The majority of citizens prefer to have their property properly protected and will support zoo directors in doing so. Vandalism can be reduced or eliminated only by means which no American zoo director appears willing or able to undertake. The prescription—

(1) Patrol of the zoo by paid or voluntary personnel during open hours and professional security guards by night.
(2) Closed-circuit television with appropriate (polite but unquestionably firm) signs on exhibits exposed to potential vandals.
(3) Barbed wire–topped fences, preferably double with a no-man's-land between them, and an electronically charged fence.

9
THE HUMAN ELEMENT

> **zoo director**—$16,000. Must possess degree in *parks management, public administration* or related field. Will be responsible for management of entire new zoo facility. Must have experience in *public relations; speech-making* necessary. (Emphasis mine)
>
> Advertisement, Raleigh, N.C., 1971

A visit to any American zoo should convince even the least discerning person of a need for improvement. Closer scrutiny will confirm that substandard conditions abound in almost every phase of zoo operation. Additional thought on the part of the individual should bring the realization that defects or inadequacies affecting captive animals can be traced to a single source—the human element.

Physical, mechanical, and engineering design problems could be eliminated, in the majority, quickly and quite easily, which would subscribe to some degree toward improvement for the animals. The major problem, unfortunately, is more serious, and has no simple solution. However well designed and built or adequate the provision for first-class maintenance of the animals, humans are needed for the zoo's efficient function, and they must be knowledgeable and competent. This cannot be expected from current zoo employees.

Few of the defects mentioned in previous chapters can be corrected without drastic revision of zoo personnel. Money, government control, or outside influence alone can accomplish little improvement; the prospect of voluntary internal overhaul is remote. Certainly, little will be done in the immediate future.

American zoos are unprofessional for diverse reasons. A dearth of personnel with any degree of expertise in fundamental zookeeping is foremost. Directors share a basic ineptitude with their lowest echelon employees. The few considered to be at the top of the zoological ladder (not actually a very high one) seem to have reached there by good luck rather than ability.

A current survey of zoo directors would show that few are qualified to train and supervise personnel, even under most favorable conditions in a new facility. A fraction of these are conversant with total zoo operation, but are so inflated by past accomplishment that they no longer give it attention. This applies especially to persons in facilities that have become so large and bureaucratic that practical zoo operation escapes them. Occupied with public speaking, writing papers, and extracurricular business or hobbies, they have no time to fulfill everyday requisites of zoo direction. Tenure makes dislodging them almost impossible, so chances for their removal are as improbable as the possibility of finding qualified successors.

Zoo directors need considerable firsthand experience with a variety of mammals, birds, and reptiles. All areas of animal husbandry, exhibit design, construction, and animal behavior, under wild and captive conditions, must be part of their training. They should be qualified to personally teach and evaluate staff, be able to make prompt, wise decisions on emergencies affecting animals, and be accountable for every activity involving physical operation of the zoo. This is a full-time occupation for a competent person.

Expertise in administrative positions is not attained overnight or by judicious delegation of work to subordinates. A good zoo director or keeper is an intelligent, hardworking, and altruistic employee.

It is customary for larger zoos to employ a veterinary as director. This classic example of bureaucratic misunderstanding has few advantages and many drawbacks. If prophylactic routines are set up and enforced by a zoo director, sickness or injury can be substantially reduced. Although zoo animals, at some time, need the skills of a veterinary, preferably one experienced with zoo animals, veterinary training alone is not qualification for direction of a zoo.

It may be interesting to know how our directors acquired their knowledge and the amount of actual apolitical experience they have. Some start at a small zoo, wait for a chance to leave it for something better, and eventually talk their way into a worthwhile job. Once there, they make certain nobody moves them. Others are inexperienced political appointees.

As they go from zoo to zoo, they take with them a few workable ideas (often the result of sacrifice of a considerable number of animals) and leave behind immovable monuments to their ineptitude. The person whose opportunity arises from the former director's departure seldom criticizes or makes improvements.

Directors undertake all kinds of projects not normally considered part of zoo management. The majority of their time is presently occupied with matters which volunteers might do better. Docent programs, education, fundraising, and handling of prospective donors have no bearing on zoo operation but are invariably associated, with detriment to the animals. Public relations, entertainment, and other activities could be carried out by volunteers under the strict supervision of a director with veto power over any activity detrimental to the zoo. There is no way to tell now whether they would do any better if all obligations other than legitimate zoo work were removed.

The first step toward improvement would be for the director to devote full-time effort in enforcing basic good zoo animal husbandry and training personnel. Someone else should be assigned to take care of matters not directly pertaining to the zoo's operation. Directors with a flair for publicity and social events could be assigned to such affairs, while someone more qualified or interested in the zoo substituted. A veterinary could advise on setting up diets and other specialized routines for the animals.

If professionalism is to be part of future zoo programs, zoo directors should be licensed by government to manage only facilities for which their ability and expertise qualifies them. The USDA is authorized by the Animal Welfare Act to evaluate and license zoo staff, but has no personnel qualified in zoo operation to do so. Their staff relies largely on zoo directors for information concerning zoo animals.

We tend to forget that most zoos, their animals, and personnel are public property or employees. The public must demand that accreditation of zoos or personnel be issued by persons other than members of the zoos' official organization, the AAZPA. It is naive nowadays to expect unbiased judgement of an individual's competence from a panel of his or her peers. There may be people in the AAZPA qualified to pass judgement, but the condition of our zoos casts doubt on their presence.

The complicated problems of zoo administration can be met only by an experienced person. The advertisement quoted at the beginning of this chapter might produce better results if the text read:

> Individual who enjoys working with nondomestic animals. Involves long hours, including weekends. Applicant must be familiar with requirements of a variety of captive wild animals, animal husbandry, and

> have extensive practical experience. Will be expected to personally train and supervise subordinates. Applicant must live on or near premises and be on call at all times, summer and winter. Needs good practical knowledge of mechanics, electricity, and equipment used in zoos, and be prepared to train personnel to maintain same. Thorough knowledge of wild animals under natural conditions; ability to detect symptoms of stress and sickness or abnormal behavior in captive animals essential. Previous experience with civil service zoo operation will not be considered. References will be investigated.

One problem remains . . . who will answer?

Most American zoo directors and an increasingly large number of "modern" zookeepers regard zoo animals as specimens, without individuality. This is to be expected, as often they are little more than entries on inventory. (In contrast, all "rejected" animals acquire a name as soon as they are on display in the "nursery." The reasons for this contradiction will remain a secret of the public relations persons who are responsible.)

American keepers are seldom permitted, much less encouraged, to treat zoo inmates as anything more than "dangerous" beasts, and have expressed this on several occasions. A San Francisco zookeeper wanted to change feeding time for leopards to suit his coffee break. "Otherwise, there's a tendency to rush it. If you don't, you'll miss coffee break. And there's terrific danger in hurrying with the leopards. That's the most dangerous string [job assigned to one person] there is."[39]

No doubt captive animals can, under certain circumstances, present a physical threat to humans, but the theory that a lone captive needs nothing more than a measured daily ration and adequate sanitation is absurd.

Our keepers have always been prevented by zoo directors from learning the advantages of tame animals common in European zoos. Directors prefer and often insist that keepers make no attempt to "tame" or form attachments to animals in the zoo. Despite many practical advantages, tameness has never been part of the American zoo.

Moving animals in our zoos is usually considered a job for the muscular, tough individual. Transfers are generally accomplished by noisy, clattering machinery brought to the site, which further alarms the animal. With proper keeper-animal rapport, stress is absent and no danger is present to either animal or employees.

U.S. zoo directors and zookeepers could learn much from their European counterparts. Fifteen years ago, Dr. H. Hediger, director of the Zurich Zoo, wrote of tame zoo animals:

> Compared with the wild state, tameness for the wild animal in captivity has only advantages. It must therefore be strongly stressed that tame animals alone should be kept in zoological gardens. . . .
>
> . . . Tameness in large animals is of great advantage when attending to them, changing their quarters, and especially when handling a number together. With animals that have no urge to escape there is no need to fear panic on such occasions, no attacks on their keepers, no attempts to break out or incidents of that sort. . . .
>
> To sum up the advantages of tameness; there are three reasons for stressing the need for tameness in as many animals as possible in zoological gardens: tameness is attractive; tameness is healthy; tameness is expedient.[40]

The professional attitude of the foreign zoo director and keeper is traditional. European zoos have their problems and many defects, but they are fortunate in enjoying a fairly reliable labor force and considerably less turnover of staff than the U.S. Choked to a lesser degree with an oversupply of college-educated unemployed, they have to contend with only a fraction of the academically trained career-oriented individuals comprising the majority of applicants for zoo work here.

It is not unusual in Europe for two generations of zookeepers to be working in the same facility. Trainees learn from the time of their engagement that zoo work is important and specialized. Keepers take pride in their job and strive to become competent and qualified. Their lives are intimately involved with the zoo—often living on the grounds with neighbors who share a common interest.

European directors are generally well versed in their profession and have spent years as keepers before promotion to directorial posts. Their competence is job security, and there is no reason to fear replacement by a more qualified person. Rather than resentment by zoo staff, they are assured of respect and support from people who know them to be capable and concerned for the zoo animals.

European keepers are encouraged to maintain a personal relationship with animals in their care, as it is considered an important association. It allows much greater awareness of the physical and mental condition of the animal; the keeper forms a bond with an individual animal which is conscious of the proximity of a trusted friend and leads a less oppressed and tedious captive life.

European zoos are not perfect; their superiority lies in practical use of years of accumulated experience, and understanding of elementary behavioral traits of individual animals. Their directors know that academic achievement is of secondary importance for the trainee keeper, and perhaps they realize that a college degree is no guarantee of individual common sense.

The San Jose, California, zoo operated on such a basis. Animals raised from infancy in captivity were, without exception, tame and tractable. Prophylactic medication was given without stress in the familiar surroundings of the exhibit. The zoo was designed for the animals, eliminating expensive restraining devices, and exhibit costs were held to a minimum. Money saved was used for purchase of items considered luxury for animals in American zoos: electric heating, humidity control, filtered salt water for marine mammals, lush landscaping, and a vandal-proof electronic security system.

Animals were transferred, when necessary, by placing a special cage by the door of their display. They entered the cage without hesitation from familiarity and trust in their human associates. Tameness facilitates moving animals when this becomes necessary.

A large elephant seal, boarded at the zoo for Marine World of Redwood City, had to be returned to the owners. On the day of its scheduled departure, Marine World was advised to pick up the animal in the late afternoon for the evening flight to Florida to minimize time in its traveling crate. The crate was placed at a convenient gate to the seal pool. Unable to wait, a crew of five stalwart men arrived at the zoo shortly before noon to take the animal. Despite my desire to transfer the animal with minimal stress, the crew decided to scare and force it into the crate. Understandably, the animal became annoyed and promptly smashed the fence made to contain it. At my insistence, the crew waited. A keeper entered the seal crate, and the animal calmly followed her into it, much to the embarrassment of Marine World's intrepid crew.

Encouragement of similar keeper-animal rapport in all zoos would reduce stress on animals and personnel. Exhibits are enhanced by animals that display interest in humans.

The civil service further contributes to mediocrity in zoo administration. Paradoxically, the city zoo director, who is responsible to the public for the management of his facility, cannot choose his own staff. Instead, staff selection is made by bureaucrats more suited by nature to paperwork than assessment of jobseekers, and at a complete disadvantage with the verbosity of the "Pepsi generation" and its misleading facade of intelligence, so many misfits are accepted.

Selection of suitable employees is difficult, as announcement of a zoo job opportunity brings startling response. Within a radius of fifty miles a stream of exotic pet owners materialize. "Animal lovers" fantasizing blissful moments fondling rejected baby animals are attracted like moths to a flame. Occasionally, individuals with some semblance of promise show up, expressing an intense interest. Lamentably, a few days' trial often reveals an irrepressible individual that may not prove an asset to the zoo. Instant experts, whose knowledge comes from books or television, are reluctant to heed advice.

Job applicants may arrive with security blankets in the shape of mothers and close friends. It is difficult to visualize them being of great help in an emergency.

Languid California residents telephone to ask about job vacancies. Examination of the "Help Wanted" columns while munching breakfast in bed is comfortable but not a sign of a highly ambitious person.

Some individuals feel they are destined to be lion tamers and will take every opportunity to demonstrate their ability in the presence of zoo visitors. They seldom make good zookeepers.

The horsey set have a congenital urge to sit on the corral (or an office chair) and "chew the fat" by the hour. This trait makes them unpopular with fellow workers whose time is occupied.

Letters from potential employees vary, but they can sometimes be a guide to character. Those beginning with a self-recommendation, backed by endless instances of achievement in rehabilitating domestic animals, must be carefully screened.

Diplomacy is needed to point out to alumnae of children's livestock clubs that the principles of raising animals for slaughter are entirely different from wild animal husbandry, which emphasizes sensible diet and living conditions contributing to long, healthy lives.

A nervous disposition is not conducive to safe zookeeping. Persons with temporary personal problems—recent or pending divorce, heavy indebtedness, or drug-associated lethargy—may prove to be good workers but should be completely recovered before they are allowed to work close to zoo animals. A keeper's concentration must be on the job.

Overweight, a common problem, is undesirable in prospective zoo employees. It is reasonable to suppose that persons incapable of taking proper care of themselves may be expected to do no better with zoo animals.

The fabled "animal person" does not exist. Some people are more suited than others to work with animals and enjoy their proximity. A surprising number will accept a job which involves extensive association with animals without having more than a passing interest in them. This, unfortunately, is true of some current zoo employees. Many keepers pass the day mechanically. Others work in zoos only for the enjoyment of being part of a public display.

Civil service personnel routinely select applicants fitting these descriptions to work in city-operated zoos, so most of them have virtually worthless employees on the payroll. Civil service trainees able to endure six months' probation become almost unfirable, and it is often easier for the supervisor to let them hide somewhere during the day.

Smaller private zoos do better with help due to the facility with which they may interview, evaluate, and hire on a trial basis. Those persons who are not considered as potential assets are terminated without repercussion. Vacancies at these places attract individuals who have confidence in their ability, which reduces screening of deadbeats and mental misfits.

Civil service cannot select personnel in this cavalier fashion: the hiring process is tedious and seldom produces satisfactory employees. The civil service is simply a haven for the insecure.

The Federal government, through the Office of Equal Employment Opportunity, forces their Robin Hood policies on city zoo directors, who are obliged to accept "workers" regardless of capability or potential. (Like many other federal programs, the EEOC's ideals are commendable but subject to chronic abuse.) This has contributed to the overwhelming difficulty of staffing an American zoo. Ironically, a small zoo (less than twenty-five employees) does not come under EEOC jurisdiction—a good reason to plan small, specialized zoos which could be operated by relatively few competent employees.

Difficulties arise from the misconception that a college diploma is automatic assurance of a well-paid position. The truth has dawned on some disillusioned unemployed graduates, but many still feel that the world owes them a living. There are more graduate incompetents than people imagine, and they are often quite untrainable, firmly believing that all necessary knowledge is part of their educational package. A couple of years of college are useful but by no means essential for a career in the zoo, where common sense and basic intelligence are of more value.

I was part of a panel of "zoo experts" to select an assistant director for the San Francisco Zoo. The panel comprised a petty city official from the personnel department, a University of California professor of biology, and the San Francisco Zoo director. Of ten applicants, all were eloquent, among them a graduate veterinary fresh from school and another whose credentials were a single experience as guide tour leader for a photo "safari." Several felt the job could be a step to a better position, two were writing theses for degrees and needed the opportunity to be with wild animals, and others were looking for a soft job.

One applicant had visited my zoo and had shown considerable interest in some of the features incorporated there. The only person who expressed interest in work with animals, my vote was cast in his favor.

The man was hired, and some time later I discovered that the zoo director had advised him to visit my zoo and show concern for zoo animals. After a comparatively short time in San Francisco, he returned to teaching. The zoo was for some time without a director or assistant, without detriment. Since this, I have become skeptical of civil service "impartial" employment procedures.

Civil service hiring practices are unsuited to zoo personnel selection. It is only logical that competent directors have free choice of prospective employees and authority to fire incompetents without interference. Until this is possible, the most able administrator can only give a mediocre performance.

The privately operated San Jose Zoo used a system in hiring that proved practical and could be used to advantage by other zoos. Advertisements were placed in local newspapers and Human Resources agencies. Text was brief and specified: "Applicant must be physically and mentally healthy. Includes weekends. Job involves non-domestic animal husbandry." Calls, answered by an automatic telephone with provision for leaving messages, eliminated persons who had no desire to work for a zoo. Messages were answered by phone the following day with a brief summary of requirements. An interview was set up for applicants who sounded reasonably sane.

The first interview was informal. Persons who were obviously unsuitable (extreme nervousness, bad job record, police record, pronounced hang-ups, and physical characteristics which could prove dangerous at work) were rejected. Most of these applicants, when work requirements were explained, agreed that other employment would be more appropriate.

Screened applicants were called later for a second interview unless they had meanwhile found other employment. Those who still expressed a desire to work were shown the zoo and told briefly what the job involved, with emphasis on the more unpleasant and tedious chores.

Interested applicants would come to the zoo for two days to observe the routine work. At 7:30 A.M. they were greeted by the pungent smell of raw horsemeat and sinks full of thawing herring. On the following day they would observe routine in the main zoo. Those considered suitable and who appeared physically capable were called about a week later and advised that they would be hired on a trial basis. At this time, the trainee was assigned to a keeper who had instructions to watch for potential problems.

During this period the new employee would not be left alone with the animals. Promising trainees were given a final interview and an opportunity to ask further question. (Regulations for employees prohibited smoking at work or on zoo grounds, long conversations with zoo visitors unless giving requested information, and visitors or phone calls unless of an emergency nature. Reasons for termination of services included loss of any animal through negligence, repeated tardiness, incompetence after completion of training, and use of drugs at work.)

Trainees who passed muster were taught standard routines for husbandry and spent one month in each phase of zoo operation before they were considered capable. Training was given by the zoo director or head keeper.

Apparently, others agreed that this system worked satisfactorily. Marvin Jones, authority on international zoos and their content, wrote an article for the *International Zoo News* regarding the San Jose Zoo:

> There is no doubt that the zoo is the cleanest that this writer has ever seen, anywhere. It is probably unique in that, with the exception of admission, nothing is sold by the zoo. There are no food stands, souvenir shops, or feeding devices. In addition, it has a staff that, with the exception of the Director, is totally female—no doubt the only zoo in the world with a 100% female work force.
>
> The animals are in top-notch physical condition and each and every cage is spick and span. While one does notice trash containers about the zoo, there is a total absence of litter on the public walkways, in the exhibits, and even in the behind-the-scenes areas. The latter are sparkling, and the off-exhibit animals are given excellent care.[41]

(Mr. Jones spent many years visiting zoos all over the world, and has accumulated a vast store of statistical knowledge that he freely shares with U.S. zoos. One of the few reliable sources for inventory information on the U.S. zoo, he lectures fairly frequently to groups of zoo directors and has set up records for better housekeeping in various facilities.)

The San Jose Zoo was an example of what may be accomplished under private management with a little effort. Prior to its phase-out, during the six months of operation (with a much larger staff) by the city of San Jose, the facility became run-down and the animals' condition deteriorated.

10

REGULATING BREEDING AND SURPLUS

> Perhaps the most outstanding achievement of last year was the receipt of an Approved Zoo Status from the United States Department of Agriculture. *This approval will enable us to import wild ruminants, such as giraffe and antelope,* and insures that we will be able to display these valuable animals *without having to rely on obtaining specimens born in captivity.*[42] (Emphasis mine)
>
> Director Robert Wagner
> Jackson Zoo, Mississippi

Results of "successful" breeding programs are evident throughout the country and in surplus zoo animal bulletins. Siberian-Bengal tiger hybrids, exhibiting some characteristics of both sub-species, are common. Many zoos label tigers Bengal or Siberian although the animals are obviously not purebred. Congenital or hereditary defects, mainly eye and skeletal abnormalities, are frequently seen but appear to present no obstacle to continued breeding by zoos. Tigers with such defects have been given to private individuals simply because the zoo could not dispose of them.

Tigers have been deliberately mated with lions, and vice versa, producing incongruous hybrids which zoo directors have classified as tigons or ligers, depending on the male parent. Hogle Zoo, Salt Lake City, displays a portrait of an earlier "success" with this abnormality in a prominent place in the feline house—appropriately close to a "Siberian" tiger display with a female tiger showing obvious signs of mixed ancestry.

Zoo-born African lions no longer look like their wild cousins. Years of zoo inbreeding have robbed them of many natural physical traits. It is possible that by now many zoo directors believe that male lions should have the facial characteristics of a St. Bernard dog. The animals have become stunted, illshapen parodies of wild lions by indiscriminate breeding serving only for overproduction of cubs for zoo nurseries.

A male lion in Manhattan Zoo, Kansas, operated under the auspices of Kansas State University, is a malformed, monstrous product of an individual's penchant for genetics. Its canine teeth removed, declawed, and castrated, this unfortunate creature is kept in a small cage for the enlightenment of local residents. One of these, taking advantage of the animal's habit of licking the wire front of its cage, amputated half of the lion's tongue with a pocket knife, to further contribute to its incredibly sad aspect.

A surplus lion was given by the San Diego Zoo to individuals who operated "Orphans of the Wild," a now-defunct California wild animal "refuge." It degenerated into a flaccid, grotesque caricature of its species, and was euthanized with several other zoo "breeding successes" in 1975.

San Francisco Zoo's jaguars produce litters year after year despite the difficulty of placing the young with other than individuals interested in "hunting." Dreadfully deformed by inbreeding and infantile malnutrition, the male, separated (far too late) from the female by a chain link fence, paces throughout the day, and each turn reveals deformed hip bones protruding at an abnormal angle from the animal's body.

Birth-control medication for lions in San Jose received considerable worldwide attention. Many letters were written by persons anxious to curtail unnecessary zoo lion births. Considerable mail came from individuals who believed that it was sadistic to deprive the cats of their "pleasure"; as most of these included offers to adopt cubs when they were born, they were not taken too seriously. No zoo director expressed interest in the program; the birth of unplaceable lions in their zoos apparently presents no problem.

A wildlife protection organization in Greece sent an approving letter but suggested that the male lion be neutered "to make him feel less frustrated." Lions, or any other animal whose sex life flourishes only when estrus occurs in a nearby female, do not—like many humans—wait impatiently for amorous adventures but are (without encouragement from the female or unless abnormal through captivity) models of celibacy.

Orangutans, labeled "vanishing" and reputedly in danger of extinction, have been routinely subjected to interbreeding in zoos. Numerous zoo orangutans are Bornean-Sumatran hybrid animals, due partly to the zoos' reluctance to loan animals of one sub-species to other zoos in possession of similar individuals. (Although after checking some orangutan facilities, it is understandable that discriminating directors would hesitate to take the risk of "loaning" to some zoos.) Another contributing factor is that few zoo directors seem to know the difference between the two sub-species, having never seen them in Borneo or Sumatra.

Great apes are becoming increasingly difficult to dispose of legally and are producing more young than there are zoos to house them. The possibility of sending them to their country of origin remains but is hardly compatible with the zoos' current practice of using animals as trading material. Possibly an organization (perhaps the United Nations) could facilitate export to countries whose natural fauna we have helped decimate: at this time it seems improbable.

By law, animals entering this country from overseas must be accompanied by documentation which testifies to species, origin, physical condition, and age. These documents are not always entirely accurate, but they are sufficient for the statistical needs of the Federal government. Once the animal is admitted it becomes a nonentity, and may be sold, bartered, donated, or dumped on any person who will take it. Failing this, it may be destroyed by anyone wishing to do so, and not necessarily in a humane manner.

Birth certificates are issued to human parents as proof of a newly born child. Throughout its entire life this document is the basis of personal identification. On demise, an equally important death certificate legalizes the citizen's departure and relieves him of any further obligations to society. Without the original document, life in a civilized country would be very complicated—although there might be some advantage to those who wish to remain incognito.

A similar system of control protecting any animal throughout its life is needed. Initially, this would entail registration of every nondomestic animal from time of zoo birth or importation. A certificate could be issued, a copy retained as permanent record for government archives, and another legally obliged to accompany the animal wherever it might be taken or kept. All pertinent data, including any issuance of offspring and their disposition, would be recorded, and information sent to the agency policing the program.

For those already in captivity, little cost would be involved. (If a wild animal must be imported, the importer would pay for initial documentation.) Zoos could have instituted a system of this nature years ago without government intervention, but have not.

The program would provide accurate statistics on zoo mortality and inventory. Abuse of surplus could more easily be controlled, and senile or unwanted stock given merciful euthanasia rather than additional trauma. Euthanasia would be performed by licensed veterinarians responsible for the authenticity of a death certificate containing facts contributing to its demise. Zoos with unduly high mortality through neglect or incompetence could be reclassified to reduce the number of animals in their possession or prohibit further acquisitions.

All movement or transfer of zoo animals could be easily traced and regulated, and records would be available to interested parties.

The procedure would obligate directors to revise husbandry programs toward conservation of their own animals. Meanwhile, with a respite from collectors and dealers, wildlife could recuperate in natural surroundings and regain balance.

Breeding should be regulated to maintain approved zoo inventories which would eliminate present surplus abuse, and eventually our zoos might become self-sufficient and make a bona fide contribution to wild animal welfare.

International controls prohibiting use of animal hides, oils, and carcasses would promptly curb further decimation by native hunters for commerce. Many countries are ready to impose controls to conserve remaining animals, and the time is ripe for an aggressive campaign.

The government, in response to pressure from wildlife and conservation groups, have realized that some concern for animals must be officially demonstrated. Bureaucrats are not well versed with animals, and progress is woefully slow. Governmental doors, however, are finally open to some means of legislating effective animal welfare.

11

GOVERNMENT AND OTHER ORGANIZATIONS

American zoo directors and staff have shown conclusively that self-policing is not enough. They have always done exactly as they pleased, and the outcome for zoo animals has been catastrophic. Zoo expertise and professional ethics, formerly unchallenged, must be subjected to controls from higher authority; regulations enforcing basic good animal husbandry legislated; and sanctions for their violation applied. The zoo director and animal dealer, naturally, unanimously denounce interference that jeopardizes a lucrative business.

It is unfortunate, but logical, that controls must be exercised through the Federal government. Some progress has been made in passage of laws which stipulate minimum physical requirements for captive animals. Zoos will have to conform to quality in order to receive the exhibitor's license essential to legal operation.

Our notoriously lethargic government has reacted only after persistent pressure from conservation and humane groups, and to these and their affiliates go the credit for legislation. Their continued efforts may prevent the new laws from being twisted into tools for unethical practice by zoos, animal dealers, and research institutions.

Zoo directors' reaction to legal controls has been predictable. Years of uninhibited authority over their domains has eliminated need for admission of error or inadequacy. Supervision is unwelcome and considered by most directors superfluous. Many feel that animal dealers should continue to ravish the dwindling supply of wild animals for replacement of zoo losses from incompetence. Dealers, obviously, share this opinion.

Legislation for animal welfare must be unmistakably in favor of the animals, and loopholes which might permit abuse of captive wild animals closed. The public must make certain that legislators are not influenced by special-interest groups, however reputable or wealthy. Animal-associated legislation is generally accomplished by effective mass public protest or lobbying by wealthy interests which include medical and biological research institutions maintained by our taxes. Zoo directors will support the strongest side to stay in business. It is up to the American taxpayer to see that all advantage goes to the animals.

There is reason to believe that zoo animals are already part of experiments conducted by laboratories; the National Zoo and New York's Bronx are active in zoo animal research.

The AAZPA, which represents American zoos, should publicly admit or deny approval and/or complicity. It is doubtful that individual zoo directors would contract with research organizations, even through dealers. All possible means must be used to bring abuses of this nature to the American people's attention. If zoos are allowed to replace the wild animal importer, public indignation may be aroused to a point which could precipitate closure of American zoos.

The U.S. Department of the Interior controls importation and transfer of animals classified "endangered" or "injurious" wildlife. Nathaniel Reed, Assistant Secretary of the Interior for Fish and Wildlife and Parks, has emphatically expressed his concern over our poor zoos, and the department has virtually stopped importation and internal transfer or sale of "endangered" species. Zoos can no longer indiscriminately trade or sell surplus of listed animals.

The new regulations are being felt by zoos that routinely dispose of surplus to the highest bidder:

> The Endangered Species Act which has proved crippling to wild animal breeders has also been felt at the Como Park Zoo in St. Paul, Minn.
>
> The zoo presently has a surplus of animals, specifically three extra jaguar cubs and a Diana monkey. The animals are crowding the permanent animals, and Como officials say their hands are tied.
>
> The law, which states that individuals cannot deal in animals for a profit, is hurting zoos, said Carlo Pyhaluoto, assistant director of the St. Paul facility. He added that much animal trade is done through private brokers and private zoo operators. "We can't always trade from zoo to zoo because the zoo that wants our animals may not have what we want."
>
> The surplus animals at Como were all bred for sale so the zoo could buy other animals. . . .
>
> The new law also makes it difficult to buy many animals, including seals, which officials say are desperately needed. "It normally takes three trained seals to put on the Sparky Show," trainer Archie Brand said, "but right now we're operating with only one." [Are the others still in the storage basement?]
>
> . . . We had requested to sell our cats to Heinz Ruhe, who operates the Children's Zoo in Oakland, Calif., Pyhaluoto said, "but, because his is a private zoo

operated to make a profit, we're being turned down by the [USDI] department."[43]

The Animal Welfare Act of 1973, a very modest animals' Bill of Rights (but a step in the right direction), is enforced by the United States Department of Agriculture. The USDA has not been noticeably active in their new role. The Animal Welfare Act cannot become effective until a serious basic problem—availability of trained personnel—is solved. Dr. Clabaugh, head of veterinary services (also an associate member of the AAZPA), may be confronted by difficulties more numerous, and possibly greater, than he anticipates.

USDA has no qualified zoo inspectors; Clabaugh must supervise training of several hundred employees in zoo operation and wild animal husbandry. Although licensed veterinarians, they are inexperienced with wild animals; most have never been closer to zoo animals than the average visitor. While training personnel of this caliber will be easier than educating laypersons, the fact that these men are distributed over the U.S. prohibits regular training. As Clabaugh does not presume to be a zoo expert, he relies to a great extent on advice from the same group that needed the legislation for animal welfare—American zoo directors.

During several hours spent with Dr. Clabaugh in 1974 discussing the future of zoos, he mentioned having watched a group of people enjoying the monkeys' antics in Central Park's second-rate menagerie, and stated his conviction that the zoo was a necessity for New Yorkers. Many people are of the opinion that amusement of the public does not justify prostitution of wild animals.

Dr. Clabaugh was given a copy of research notes and tentative chapters for this book in the hope that they might be of use to his inspectors. Some months later he wrote a letter acknowledging some "useful content." Apparently under the impression that the notes comprised the entire book, Clabaugh noted that it was too negative, and if authentic, suggested that few well-run zoos existed. This was precisely my intention; no other conclusion could be truthfully reached.

According to United Action for Animals, a New York based organization dedicated primarily to promoting public awareness of vivisection on zoo animals, the Animal Welfare Act may not be what it seems. UAA has done considerable research, and makes a valid case for close watch on the USDA, USDI, and legislators who try to bulldoze researcher-sponsored bills. Those bills, says UAA, will protect the animals only while in the zoo, but not when they leave the facility. Their pamphlets quote Omaha Zoo director Lee Simmons as offering surplus primates (free) to primate researchers, and an announcement in the Laboratory Primate Newsletter where the El Paso Zoo advertises a number of rhesus monkeys for disposal.[44]

Hunting zoo-originated hoofed stock on game ranches is common and becoming more prevalent. Ranch operators make up to 500 percent profit on a live animal when hunters kill it for a trophy. It will be difficult to persuade them to desist. Offering a "guaranteed hunt" featuring blackbuck, aoudad, axis deer, sika deer, and other exotic wall adornments at any time of year, the ranches operate within state laws; the USDA Animal Welfare Act does not protect these animals and cannot stop them. Zoos must not be allowed to further this activity by overbreeding, although zoo directors with a penchant for hooved stock realized the potential big business opportunities with ungulates—especially rare ones—long ago. It is only a matter of time before lions and other big game animals are on the ranches' hunting lists.

The zoos' unhappy situation has been brought about by years of lax direction. Now, pressure from all sides is bringing to light facts about captive wild animals people never dreamed of, and many more will erupt.

In the meantime, hundreds of zoo animals remain in

conditions which, if imposed upon domestic animals, would land the person responsible in a court of law. Languishing in inadequate, dark cells, they are tended by semi-trained personnel whose criteria for captive animal care is in birth statistics to inflate their zoo's prestige. Nothing is being done toward reducing the unnecessary loss of life in our zoos; until it is, responsibility for all untimely animal deaths lies squarely with the individual zoo director.

Among the many humane, conservation, wildlife protection, and animal rescue agencies are many sincere people. A number of blatant opportunists have joined them and show remarkable talent in feathering their own nests. A few make a comfortable living for themselves and their disciples while "saving" wildlife from harm by other humans.

The need for an everincreasing rapport with these organizations is worrying unscrupulous zoo directors. Some scrupulous employees of these humane groups, taking advantage of public support and funds, have discovered this and combine entertainment with development of social status through their work.

All animal protection organizations have a common creed of concern for wildlife and domestic stock. It is strange that even token fellowship between groups is so conspicuously absent, and rivalry in organizations with similar goals so bitter and intense.

Heading the list of vociferous defenders of animals is the Humane Society of the United States (HSUS). From headquarters occupying an entire building in Washington, D.C., a steady flow of well-prepared pamphlets, bulletins, and newsletters, all appealing for donations, are mailed to citizens throughout the country.

Sue Pressman, an HSUS zoo investigator (who according to some zoo officials occasionally borrows the title "Doctor") was formerly an apprentice keeper in Boston's old zoo. Conflicting stories on the transition from trainee zoo help to HSUS official zoological expert vary with their location and source. One thing is certain—Pressman is the bête noire of the U.S. zoo. Feared by directors of mediocre establishments, and despised by others who maintain a professional level of operation, Pressman is as welcome in most zoos as an anthrax epidemic and appears to be almost as difficult to eradicate.

Their attitude is understandable; Pressman's forte lies in occasional visits to facilities whose director may not meet with her approval. These visits are followed by demands for change that often involve needless major investments or are impossible to meet.

Ms. Pressman's public statements with regard to some zoos are not always accurate and sometimes reveal a lamentable dearth of professionalism. HSUS modestly claims that through her intervention scarcely a week passes that zoos are not forced to close or a director is fired,[45] which is not true and would hardly be a practical solution if it were; someone equally incompetent would take over.

Roger Caras, a curiously flexible anti-zoo writer and a vice-president of the HSUS, was among those who lambasted the Central Park Zoo for its treatment of animals. His criticism has declined noticeably since his liaison with the City of New York, which pays a sizable sum for advice on its zoo housekeeping improvements. While Caras's books featuring wildlife, and TV appearances with young animals borrowed from local zoos may be entertaining, his experience hardly qualifies him as an expert on zoo design or captive animals. It is possible that Caras's association with the HSUS expedited the appointment.

The HSUS has spared no effort to publicize its heroic role in "investigating" zoos. Their March 1975 bulletin's "Special Report on Zoo Reform" is the culmination and summary of a campaign against conditions in zoos. Large headlines proclaim:

> HSUS has succeeded in bringing the plight of zoo animals to the attention of all Americans. [This is nonsense; many wildlife organizations with far less working capital have been saying for years that zoo animals are badly kept, but were less concerned with personal publicity.] The Humane Society of the United States has taken the lead for the past 3½ years in reforming American zoos. [Perhaps this implies that prior to that time zoos were different.] In some cases, the zoos were permanently closed and HSUS coordinated arrangements for removing the animals to more humane quarters. . . .
>
> . . . HSUS has been responsible for relocating bears from a roadside bar and grill in South Carolina, an Ohio riding stable, and an auction house in Florida to natural habitat surroundings.[46]

HSUS's conception of natural habitat is unusual. The Ohio bear was sent to Orphans of the Wild in Buellton, California, where it was kept in a barred cage fifteen by twenty-five by eight feet with an open-ended shelter on a concrete floor until the owners were evicted from the property after two years of nonpayment of rent. HSUS's approval of the foster home shows hasty and poor judgment: the animal was not mutilated in any manner and could later have been released in a wilderness area near Ohio.

The report continues:

> Roger Caras, an HSUS vice-president, was commissioned by New York City to conduct a study of the New York City zoos after severe criticism of the zoos by HSUS and other organizations.
>
> Nevertheless, the amount of money needed to transform major zoos into humane facilities is enormous.[47]

Mr. Caras's association with the City of New York has already been mentioned; it may not be entirely altruistic, and will contribute to the high cost of reform.

Pressman, quoted in a Philadelphia newspaper as "director of wildlife protection" for the HSUS, praised drive-through animal parks: "The animals are free to roam and set up territories. They can act as they do in the wild."[48] Apparently she was unaware of the high mortality during initial territorial disputes. In contradiction, the March bulletin reads:

> While it had been widely assumed that ride-through or drive-through zoos would be an improvement over traditional zoos, it hasn't turned out that way.[49]

In another bulletin, headlines proclaim: "Pressman trains USDA." For a successful future of the Animal Welfare Act it can only be hoped that preparation of Federal animal welfare inspectors will include instruction from people more fully versed with facts on zoos.

HSUS's bulletins have two definite themes: the HSUS is the first and best organization, and most concerned about captive animals; HSUS needs money—lots of it. The former is not true; many persons have been aware of the zoo situation and have spent a lot of their own money and time trying to improve it. The latter is factual; HSUS pays its staff well, and overhead expenses to support a building in Washington (with plush offices and numerous personnel) are high.

Hostility betweeen HSUS and other organizations of a similar nature may be heightened by HSUS's sanctimonious attitude. The smaller groups rely largely on small donations from members; some of them do not solicit funds at all other than a minimal membership fee. It is natural that some resentment should be felt, considering HSUS's lavish budget for the same objectives.

In July 1974 the director of the HSUS, John Hoyt, was given a condensation of notes, made during our research trip, on defects affecting the well-being of zoo animals to assist Ms. Pressman in her investigations. I left his office under the impression that the voluntary contribution was considered possible competition rather than helpful. (When contacted by phone from California, Mr. Hoyt expressed surprise that I should wish to donate the research material.)

Humane and conservation organizations would do well to divert more effort toward a united front. The distressing absence of cooperation between these well-meaning groups robs them of what might be an immensely powerful weapon against abuse of wild animals. Nevertheless, they have accomplished a great deal. It is unfortunate that except in one or two instances their founders have become insufferable bores who seem unable to accept the viewpoint of others, and fail to recognize that compromise is often a necessary part of progress.

HSUS and USDA programs cannot be effective in controlling abuse until their inspectors have acquired the expertise to recognize defects in husbandry without help from zoo operators and will devote full time to unannounced physical checks of premises.

12

EVALUATING YOUR LOCAL ZOO

On your next visit to a zoo, look beyond the public relations brochures and "endangered species" signs, and check the following:

Are pens and cages of adequate size; can the animals walk at least four times their own length?

Does the animal have free access to sanctuary from visitors; is there a "den" in the cage? (Or are inside shelter doors closed; no box or den provided?)

Do "daytime" animals have adequate light and/or sun? (Or are they in dark interior cages with no access to outside runs or U/V light?)

Is food eaten promptly at feeding time? (Or is there leftover food on floors and dishes?)

Are cages clean and sanitary? (Or are stools and urine on the floor; are stools loose?)

Are the animals at the front of the cage, and do they appear alert and relaxed? (Or are they curled up near the back of the exhibit, or pacing nervously?)

Are birds in open areas able to fly? (Or are their wings pinioned—look for short wings when they stretch?)

Do birds in aviaries have ample flight space and height? (Or are perches difficult to reach except by helicopter?)

Do cages or dens have artificial heat or cooling installed; on a warm day do animals breath normally?

Do all animals have free access to a choice of heat, shade, light?

Are marine mammals kept in salt water; are the pools large, round or oval, and with adequate haul-out space, and a suitable color? (Or does the color of the pool reflect sunlight?) Is the water absolutely clear and clean? (Or are fish and debris floating on top or bottom?)

Are sea lions active and alert? (Discount visitor-fed seals begging.) Are they fed by hand, individually? (Or is fish thrown to them in the pool?) Are their eyes a dark, lustrous brown? (Or are they closed, slightly closed, or opaque bluish-white?) Do they appear to be in general good condition? (They should look rubbery with no visible vertebrae or ribs.)

Do animals that naturally dig in the earth have a floor which permits this activity? (Or are they on concrete, bricks, tile, or other synthetic material?)

Is there clean drinking water, free of algae and debris, in all cages?

Are nocturnal animals able to avoid direct or bright light?

Are young animals with parents? (Or labeled "rejected" in a glass-fronted nursery?)

Do the hoofed animals walk easily? (Or do they look like they're wearing snowshoes?)

Are great apes active? Do they have company and things to do? (Or are they in small pens, alone, with nothing to do but sleep and eat?)

Are keepers close to animal exhibits, supervising visitors? Are they working? On what?

Do elephants and other large animals have rubbing posts or mounds in their pens?

Are bars or other restraint methods safe? (Or are there sharp spikes or other fixtures which might harm the animals?)

If exhibits are water-moated, are there visible means of escape for animals should they fall in?

Do dry-moated exhibits have a heavy layer of soft material (hay, straw, etc.) to protect animals if they fall?

Do birds have at least two separate perches or roosts? (Or can they fly only into walls, fences, or floor if frightened?)

The first part of each question should be answered YES. If this is not so, ask to see the zoo director or his assistant—not the public relations person or "educational curator"—and ask WHY; then brace yourself for evasive answers or rhetoric.

If you were able to answer YES to every question, you are the zoo PR person or your eyesight is failing. Take a closer look!

13
THE FUTURE

If the nation's zoos were miraculously renovated and entirely suited to captive animals, little improvement in their care could be expected until staff was properly trained. Currently, there are not enough qualified persons to maintain a quarter of America's zoos.

A practical solution might be to restrict the size of zoos to fit availability of professional personnel. This would involve consideration of species to be housed, with careful matching of animals to climatic conditions and available facilities. The small, specialized zoo might solve the basic personnel problem, but no improvement can be expected until professionalism becomes mandatory. Until zoos are run by persons who understand and dedicate themselves to captive animals, their continuance cannot be justified.

Most directors view innovations with suspicion; changes that might affect their careers will be additionally hard to make, so public pressure will be needed to initiate training and licensing programs.

Zookeeping must be learned in a professional manner—a disciplined, practical study program culminating with internship under zoo working conditions. We cannot expect any degree of success with crash training programs.

There are currently no training schools for zoo personnel. Moorpark College's (California) two-year course on wild animal husbandry and handling (with the emphasis on animal training, unfortunately) may be a start. A visit to the campus in August 1975 was not encouraging, and the course material leans more toward therapy for the would-be movie star and other *homo neuroticus*. Obviously, standards of zookeeping techniques must be established before schools on a large scale can become uniformly effective. These standards must be far more comprehensive than the USDA's present criteria for animal welfare.

Many groups and individuals believe in phasing all zoos out. It must be remembered that there are currently about 130,000 animals already in our zoos; phasing out zoos would not eliminate their problems. Something must be done with them—mass euthanasia would seem most inappropriate. Unfortunately, many revolutionary ideas are impractical: it is better to accept the fact that zoos are here; take steps to improve them and protect zoo animals from additional human ignorance or neglect; enforce stricter operating regulations; and insist on legislation prohibiting their use for experiments or research in or outside the zoo.

Substantial improvement could be made if all public zoos were removed from civil service control, placed under contract operation to nonprofit societies, and funded by the Federal government. Zoos should not be obliged to beg for operating funds or rely on money from social activities and advertising. Federal financial support is probably the only satisfactory fiscal solution—bearing in mind that financial support need not involve Federal operation; management must be left to licensed professionals.

It is too late to lament the decimation of wildlife; we must discontinue activities which contribute to further wild animal losses. First, importation of wild animals must stop.

The ensuing respite from collectors would give remaining animals a chance to achieve a natural balance in suitable areas set aside and financed by international wildlife protection funds.

Selective breeding to replace senile animals, and birth-control programs to prevent overpopulation, must be part of the future zoo's program. Zoo animals must not be indiscriminately bred for sale to game ranches, researchers, and charlatans.

Constant policing of all areas of zoo operation by the public and government departments involved with animal welfare will be essential to ensure progress for the animals in American zoos.

APPENDIXES

APPENDIX I
BRIEF NOTES ON U.S. ZOOS (January-May 1974)

ALABAMA, BIRMINGHAM

Keeper washing polar bears' grottos threw powdered HTH chlorine on exhibit; wind was blowing same on visitors and bears. Residual chlorine-water washed into moat occupied by one bear. Bears showed signs of discomfort from fumes, and animal in moat could have burned feet.

Artificial turf used on floor of small mammal cages takes time to dry, leaving cats and other mammals without dry places to stand or rest.

Inside aviary for egrets, spoonbills, etc. had roost branch too high. Not enough running space for birds to reach it easily, which could cause damage to necks/legs.

Drain gratings in small mammal exhibits hazardous to animals in panic situation (hose-down, for example).

Polished tile floor in large cat house slippery. (Keeper used Ajax or other soap for cleaning.)

Leopard died of starvation before director decided that Zupreme was no good—they are now feeding horsemeat (keeper).

Giraffe indoor house floor slippery from excrement and urine.

All indoor exhibits smelt strongly of urine and excrement—should use chlorinated hose-down water.

Catta lemur gave birth to twins while we were present. No separate quarters were provided for her; other lemurs could damage young.

Crippled ocelot in children's zoo should be euthanized—it can barely walk.

Cages for hawks, cara cara, eagles too small.

Cramped and overcrowded bobcats (five in one exhibit).

Outdoor cages for cats 20 feet below visitor eye level. Will be very hot in summer.

Sloping roof and front on flight cage reduces flight space considerably.

Fairy castles on islands not easy to clean.

Bars on orang cages too close together.

Water in exhibits dirty, much algae.

Signs with "Zoo Improvements" for 1971 still present. Also "Beautification Award for 1971."

ALABAMA, MONTGOMERY

Small cages for owls with mesh floor unsuitable for these birds.

Golden eagles in pre-fab cage—no guard rail.

Small (5' x 6') cages for crested porcupine and macaques.

Educational signs in contrast to exhibits: "African lion, Habitat—veldt and open space." Exhibit is a 10'x10' concrete-floored cage.

Good-sized aviary with buzzards, king vulture, and some smaller birds.

ARIZONA, PHOENIX

Mountain lions, wolves, foxes, bobcats behind glass without retiring space. All actively pacing.

Small aviaries around zoo poorly designed with metal roofs. Capuchins housed similarly. (Temperature reaches 20–120°). All are rusty and need painting.

Hawks tethered to tree stumps.

Owls behind glass without hiding place and overcrowded.

Minimal information on signs.

ARIZONA, TUCSON
Arizona Senora Desert Museum

Display indigenous animals only.

Exhibits done very well except birds: their cages were rusty and too small.

Otter and beaver exhibits very well done.

Design of burrows well done, with one-way glass and red lights to avoid startling occupants.

ARIZONA, TUCSON
Randolph Park

Attempts to screen cages with trees improve what would otherwise be simply an animal holding compound. Exhibits were fair to bad, with the exception of a walk-through aviary which was planted by keepers.

Seals in filtered, fresh water. Filtration equipment occupies 30 percent of exhibit space. Should be for salt water operation.

Wanderoo with central nervous system problem.

Some open exhibits were well planted, especially one with Bornean fireback pheasant.

A great deal of chain link is used to remind us this zoo belongs to city.

ARKANSAS, LITTLE ROCK

Chimp island (one of few in U.S.) was grey concrete. Access to service through long tunnel which showed considerable seepage from water pressure above. Whole exhibit presented cold, damp aspect (winter).

Cats' housing poor (10' x 10') for such animals as Siberian tigers. One tiger with amputated tail and spinal injury, very lame.

Overcrowded raccoons (seven) on concrete floor in grotto.

Two jaguarondis on a stainless steel-floored pen—hardly biological surface.

Wolves in grotto being hosed down by keeper were upset by his presence and noise of water.

Anteaters on concrete floor.

Very little sunlight available for monkeys.

Bear moats full of garbage.

Airplane displayed by aviary for some reason.

Albino dingos with puppies promise source for other zoos to perpetuate these freaks.

CALIFORNIA, COARSEGOLD
Yosemite Wild Animal Park

Spartan housing; exhibition and maintenance of animals poor.

Entire operation demonstrates frugality, minimal animal husbandry, and lack of expertise.

Tiger exhibited with lions (it has killed one lion and one female tiger).

Macaques, baboons, and bears do not make good neighbors, and spend much time running from each other. (Driver of train emphasizes that this is fun to watch.)

Stripped to the wood, trees do not provide any shelter from sun or rain; metal oil drums do little to ease cold or heat.

Hippo pool overflow is diverted through other animal pens whose occupants drink from it.

CALIFORNIA, FOLSOM CITY

Several comparatively small chain link cages provide several small mammals, including albino raccoon, a home. Fortunately, the collection is small.

A small padlocked box asks for money "To help feed the animals." Little footprints leading to this box are painted on the walkway, presumably to encourage those who cannot read to stumble over and drop a coin.

CALIFORNIA, FRESNO

Metal climbing bars in monkey cages not good for animals (too hot-cold, slippery when wet).

Public contact with orangs possible—both orangs had bubble gum.

Zupreme on floor of many cages several hours after feeding—many flies around.

Muntjac and adjoining pens had automatic water bowls—all filthy and algae covered.

Many extrusions on inside of pens/cages.

Badger on concrete 4' x 4' pen.

Walkway for visitors drains into hippo area.

Rhino deaths—two in one year. Galapagos tortoise same—from cold.

Sea lions in fresh water.

Horned owls displayed with hawks.

Cats' outside runs should be half-covered on roof for sunshade/rain shield.

California, Lodi

Seal pool empty—high mortality—fresh water.

African lion with untreated open sores on rear. Three lion cubs on surplus.

Jaguar cubs routinely sold to public for cash. Pair sold to Norco of trophy fame.

Chains on monkey island dangerous to animals' fingers. Rope should be used.

Flamingos exposed to loud noise from concession rides next door. Should be screened—injury could result from fright.

Dog pound-sized runs for coyote, wolves.

Cacomistle exposed to sunlight in small brick cubicle.

California, Los Angeles

Seals in fresh water. Leftover fish on land and in pools. Should be handfed ration.

Sloths exposed to heat-lamp burns.

Jaguarondi's fur removed by friction while pacing.

No hiding places for most animals housed in glass-fronted exhibits.

Aviary heaters installed but not working.

Most outdoor exhibits were barren and viewed from above. Many inside pens were dirty, poorly landscaped, and unattractive.

CALIFORNIA, MERCED

Leopards' cage small and in sun.

Wolf and coyotes in 12' x 8' pen.

Technical names on plates for animals are out of place in this small menagerie.

CALIFORNIA, OAKLAND
Knowland Park

Chimpanzees overcrowded—three adults in medium-sized cage (all are neurotic, ex-research animals).

Lions locked out of shelter during day—sleeping quarters offer no privacy to animals.

Sun bears overfed and inadequately housed (200 sq. ft.); same lack of privacy as lions. (These exhibits are identical.)

Gibbon cage poor design, difficult maintenance, hazardous to stock. Many gibbons lost (thirty) here during five years due to falls.

Numerous self-praise signs at gate—animal information signs poor.

CALIFORNIA, OAKLAND
Oakland Baby Zoo

Lion cubs used for display should be fed by mother until weaned.

Harbor seal in dirty fresh water, no swimming space, water contaminated from bird ponds before reaching seal.

Sea lions mutilated to prevent damage to feeding public (teeth removed), and are in fresh opaque water. Filters were not working although these could provide saline. (Porpoise/seal mortality high.)

California, Riverside
Ron's Children's Zoo

Mountain lion, wolf cages small (7' x 7'), dirty, and dark; small mesh chicken wire inadequate. No water in drinking bowls; fed pigeons with feathers; very dirty floor and cages.

Wallabies have insufficient shelter, no water to drink.

Baby Asian elephant died from OD Seconal given by visitor.

Celebes ape with chronic nervous disorder—apparently for five years duration. Should be euthanized.

Alligator "storage" (under barn) cold and dirty.

Owner and operator had no training in husbandry; used stock as gimmick for pet shop, and AAZPA as means to keep prohibited fish.

California, Sacramento

High mortality of marine mammals—one left, April 1974.

Heat lamps in cat shelters behind wire screen are burn and shock hazard to animals.

Heat lamps for anacondas are burn hazard; large 4" diameter rocks from beach unbiological for them.

Elephant exposed to wrongly installed chain link fence when taking food from visitors; dangerous angle iron in pen.

Otter pool color will damage eyes or cause discomfort; much algae.

Public feeding prevalent. School groups poorly chaperoned, feeding junk from lunch bags to animals. No signs prohibiting feeding.

Albino raccoon breeding with normal specimen.

Too much space occupied by tigers' moat—leaves little floor space for animals.

Sea lion pool has little space for haul-out by pool (maximum 6'); animals cannot rest on land without close proximity to public.

Many "endangered" signs with pictures—animal identification average.

CALIFORNIA, SAN DIEGO

Huge, overcrowded "holding compound" built in an attractively planted park.

Many exhibits, especially those for many birds, small, without shade facility or hiding places. Many birds in unbiological cages.

Repetitious ungulate pens have many protrusions from concrete walls.

"Canine row" exhibits almost identical, concrete steps; dogs pacing. "Cat row" same but with standard concrete trees.

Seals in fresh water—fur seal, elephant seal, grey seal—eye problems universal. Surplus fish in water.

Primates housing basic—small cubicles with concrete tree (smaller version of those used for cats).

Vending machines, snack shacks invite public feeding of unsuitable food.

Too much traffic in zoo—pick-up trucks, buses, etc.

"Endangered" and "Vanishing Animal" signs everywhere. Contradictory information: "Habitat forest"—exhibit with bare dirt or concrete floor without hiding place.

CALIFORNIA, SAN FRANCISCO

Monkeys and other small mammals not provided with adequate shelters; sometimes only half of a metal oil drum.

Seals in fresh water; public feeding; some with eye problems.

Very old, degenerated lion still being exhibited. Should either be euthanized or removed to off-exhibit quarters with straw bedding.

CALIFORNIA, SAN JOSE
San Jose Baby Zoo

Seals (fur and harbor) in fresh, dirty water—paper cups, etc.; public feeding allowed. Salt water filtration available but not in use.

Lion's drinking water dirty, algae covered.

CALIFORNIA, SANTA BARBARA

Small, well-kept zoo. Capybara exhibit contains a clean water pool, grass, bushes and shelter for occupants. Lion exhibit also well thought out.

Sea lion pool adequate except for salt water filtration facilities.

Asian elephants in top condition and provided with well-designed exhibit.

COLORADO, COLORADO SPRINGS

Giraffes had overgrown hooves (five of twenty-three); inside entrance door inadequate (too narrow) for so many animals.

Holes and cracks in floors of vulture/eagle cages with green drinking water; down-turned spiked rail too close to roosting perches.

Many flies, no pest control. (Maintenance curator said no deaths attributable to flies noted, so no control.)

Three echidnas on concrete 3' x 3' glass-fronted pen with small amount of straw.

Sumatran male tiger with marked ricket/skeletal problem walked with difficulty.

Slick floor from water on young orang colony, with deep moat dangerous. Fiberglass trees also slippery (one animal fell while we watched).

Cats' indoor pens (12' x 9') could be larger.

Birdhouse had bad mildew odor. Needs ventilation and/or fungicidal treatment during cleaning. Tiles of birdcage walls unsuitable. No source of sunlight in bird exhibits other than rain forest which included outside facility.

Education building quite elaborate. Nominal signing for animal exhibits.

COLORADO, DENVER

Small mammals, especially spider monkeys, crowded.

Primate house dark; orangs' ceiling 8 feet high—too low.

Giraffes' outside area rail hazardous in panic situation; also has sharp angle corner at one end.

Overhanging rocks on tiger moat could be dangerous to animals (falling into moat). Cats' indoor exhibits tiled and small. Zupreme surplus on floor of all cat cages. Three lions slept with much of this in cage. (Keeper: "It prevents cats from fighting over food.")

Sea lions in fresh water; exhibit shape poor, no filtration or provision for salt.

Eagles in small low runs like pheasants.

Old greenhouse serving as aviary—run-down paint, dirty glass, lots of algae. (New bird exhibit being built)

Poor choice of colors in rhino/hippo inside building.

Attractive emu/kangaroo display included an old log house for indoor quarters; it blended with grassed exhibit well.

Open areas for ungulates are ample, well designed.

COLORADO, PUEBLO

Uneaten Zupreme everywhere inside cat/monkey house.

European bear very thin, neurotic; labeled "KILLER."

Dingo pit full of debris, garbage, dirty water.

Hawks housed with owls.

General run-down condition for all exhibits. Saw no keepers anywhere in zoo.

Drive-through arrangement for ungulate viewing, plus car parking in front of exhibits poor. No security—dogs and other animals can enter zoo.

The large monkey island with 10-foot moat is marred by a lighthouse and concrete boat in a shipwrecked condition. (It would be advantageous to the public and a kindness to the animals if a larger boat could be provided for the inhabitants which might embark on a one-way voyage—past the lighthouse—and out to sea.)

CONNECTICUT, BRIDGEPORT

Three coyotes in outside pen without shelter outside. Stone den wet and dirty. All outside pens lacked weather protection.

Two buzzards in cage with improperly placed roost perch, completely waterlogged (rain/sleet).

Great anteater in small concrete-floored pen.

Shelter floor of bear exhibit too low—flooded or wet when raining.

Half a perimeter fence protects the zoo from vandalism (we can only hope this is reduced by 50 percent).

CONNECTICUT, NEW LONDON

No perimeter security fence.

Bird exhibits provide no shelter for occupants—eagle without shelter, waterlogged.

Generally dirty, run-down pens. A thorough cleaning plus shelters would improve this zoo 100 percent, which would bring it up to substandard conditions.

DISTRICT OF COLUMBIA

Sea lion in bear exhibit (barred and spiked); fresh water.

Anteater on concrete with sawdust, behind glass. Most small mammals housed similarly, some without the sawdust; unbiological quarters.

Rhino with rubbed-off horn from poor design of bars.

Hippo quarters very small (inside); some problems with power-operated doors.

Lame Père David's deer—rocks and loose earth.

"To Panda" signs at every available corner.

FLORIDA, JACKSONVILLE

Emus knee-deep in water puddle at "African Feeding Station." Public feeding popcorn and peanuts everywhere.

Seals in fresh water—eyes bad.

Bear grottos too deep, platform provided for viewing shows lack of planning.

Frequent PA announcements of "Chimp Show."

FLORIDA, MIAMI

Monkeys poorly housed—no shelters.

Garbage in alligator pools and all water exhibits.

Generally run-down.

FLORIDA, WEST PALM BEACH

Two coatimundis in 4' x 4' x 6' cage. Binturong in same.

Tapir in dirty water (one already died).

Poor choice of animals for this small zoo: tapirs, elephants, etc.

GEORGIA, ATLANTA

Eroded soil is part of most open exhibits, while "war time" camouflage effect of the backdrop/dividing walls is less than aesthetically perfect.

Elephant has large outdoor and odorous indoor house, without a rubbing post or trees. Gravel surface could cause some trouble. Rhinos share same needs; had too many rocks to be comfortable.

Inside cat cages small (10' x 8'), made cats appear unusually large. Cats overweight. Polished red tile floor unbiological.

Gorilla pen small and barred; one animal has lived thirteen years in exhibit (keeper).

Sea lion pool has no provision for filtration, saline; dirty water.

Outside tiger area loses much floor area to pool, bridge, etc.

Merry-go-round in zoo exhibit area—loud noise.

Old Kodiak bear sold to game farm for hunting—$50 (keeper).

IDAHO, BOISE

Small well-kept zoo; with few exceptions, exhibits are adequate and attractive.

Faulty negative slope on wire mesh denuded two macaques. (Shelf badly located makes contact rub skin excessively; fur returned when animals were temporarily placed in normal cage.)

Small, cylindrical cages for screech owl and sparrow hawk; visitors can surround cages on all sides. Ornamental metal perches not good for birds' feet.

Badger exhibit good; dirty floor enabled burrowing. (Restraining wall too low, however.)

Porcupine, beaver had grass, trees, places to hide.

Cats had trees and open shelters (mountain lions).

ILLINOIS, BLOOMINGTON

Dark interior for all exhibits. No provision for sunlight or substitute.

Seals housed in 14 foot diameter pool inside; fresh water, lights shine down on pool from center. No haul-out space. No provision for filtration/salt.

Glass-fronted display for white-tailed deer, hazardous.

ILLINOIS, CHICAGO
Lincoln Park

New seal pool filtered, but fresh water.

Orang exhibit cramped, two animals in 8' x 10' cage.

Bird house exhibits dark. No provision for sunlight.

Children's zoo small pens out of context with rest of zoo.

Elephant's foot trash container in one administrative office; doubtful value, bad taste for conservation-conscious zoo.

ILLINOIS, MOLINE

Cats inside in small 7' x 7' cages—no outside runs.

Four spider monkeys in 4' x 5' x 5' cage.

Peccaries in water/mud 6' x 9' corral.

Eagles' (amputated wings) roost perch too high for easy access. Circular cage without guard rail allows visitors to get too close to birds.

Aoudads' hooves overgrown badly.

Groundhogs shown in concrete-floored pit.

Lion cubs given to drive-through died in one month.

Two neurotic adult chimps housed in typical indoor cage.

ILLINOIS, SPRINGFIELD

Guard rails around most exhibits too low.

Pre-fab cages not bad; one contained wolf with deformed foot—probably due to rickets when cub.

INDIANA, EVANSVILLE

Heavy algae growth in pools and exhibits, plus sign saying how nice to have it.

Generally run-down; much trash in exhibits, walkways.

Indoor house for birds has cold air ducts in rear of each exhibit. Air current would be hazardous to occupants (curator reported 60 percent loss of stock in first year of use).

INDIANA, INDIANAPOLIS

Costly entrance motif not compatible with zoo.

Indian temple on elephant exhibit housing African species. Elephant was too close to visitors who were feeding popcorn and foil to occupant.

Excellent tiger exhibit provides grass, trees, pool.

Giraffe stabbed with pitchfork by visitor—vandalism high (keeper).

IOWA, DES MOINES

Animals overweight; surplus Zupreme on floor (director's orders).

Young Asian elephant's trunk extremity badly torn and left to heal (housed next to jaguar that tore it).

Winter storage quarters a firetrap (had caught fire once); rat infested and dirty.

Director public relations man: see *Man in a Cage* by Robert Elgin.

IOWA, MUSCATINE

Tiger from Des Moines Zoo in small cage. Feet very sore from walking on cold, wet concrete (alkaline burns).

Three neurotic semi-adult chimps in "storage" small cage; baby behind glass (4' x 4' x 4') exhibit.

Two lions in small cage, but heated.

Macaques in unheated brick exhibit.

KANSAS, GARDEN CITY

Open to all traffic until 11:00 P.M.; drive-in, dogs allowed, parking in front of exhibits. A sign, however, prohibits camping in the zoo.

Seals have been killed by rubber balls, etc. thrown in fresh water pool (frequent visitor).

Polar bear killed by police when let out of cage. No security (frequent visitor).

No visible attendants in zoo.

KANSAS, GREAT BEND

High sea lion mortality—pool empty, fresh water.

Poor choice of colors in zoo—bright blue, pink, green.

Education building superior to most exhibits.

KANSAS, MANHATTAN

Male lion should be euthanized (castrated, declawed, canine teeth ground off, and tongue cut off by visitor).

Security rails insufficient for cats.

Dingos, foxes, and coyotes behind chicken wire without security rail for visitors.

Jaguar very overweight.

New arrival (leopard) housed next to tiger and lions, very nervous from neighbors' proximity.

No supervision of public: visitors climbed safety rail to feed tiger, leopard grass, etc.

Zoo maintained by University of Kansas.

KANSAS, TOPEKA

Glass-fronted cassowary pen with slick concrete and straw hazardous to birds.

Alligator pool dangerous for visitors; could reach animals from bridge.

Orang smearing feces on window glass.

Cages for eagles have no overhead cover or shelter.

Tamandua in new "rain forest" on concrete with spilled, improperly blended food. Had no commercial blender (assistant director). (Building's roof dome alone cost $100,000.)

Gorilla exhibit 12' x 12' inside.

Rain forest showy structure but full of poor design features: noisy fans for cooling/circulation destroy rain forest atmosphere. Small enclosures for margay, etc. will be damp and inadequate for occupants. Manually operated weather-temperature-humidity panels should be automated. Will require constant manual changes by operator to suit conditions outside.

Polar bear cages formed in half circle; this reduces space for animals.

KANSAS, WICHITA

Extrusions from exhibit dividers can be hazardous to animals.

Chain link fence (6 feet) covered by water in moat has danger potential for horned animals should they go into water, especially wildebeest, etc.

Lion and tiger exhibits, perhaps patterned after the tiger exhibit in Indianapolis, are good; dirt surfaces and large area.

Kentucky, Louisville

Most attractive and functional zoo seen. Adequate, well-planned grounds, inside and outside housing are credit to the director, who did much of basic design. (Dr. Poglayan was terminated by the zoo board because of his insistence on high-quality exhibits for zoo animals.)

All exhibits are large and conditions of all specimens very good.

Excellent cheetah display on grassy hillside is masterpiece of simplicity and economy with maximum conditions for occupants.

Very nice monkey island; had electric restraint wires—not usual single wire which could be fatal if touched by animal in water but an insulated double pole arrangement.

Louisiana, Alexandria

Black bear in small cage has rectal prolapse, needs attention. No shelter.

Five lions in small cage; no wind shield.

Keeper giving private "contact" visits to people; no trained personnel.

Badger in filthy cage; no wind shield.

Small wheeled circus cages much too small.

Bengal tiger in cramped quarters.

Bobcat in water from leaking hose nearby; unable to find dry place.

Entire park run-down and in disorder. Water around monkey island very dirty.

Everything here for discriminating zoo visitors: merry-go-round, rides, hot dogs, etc.

No perimeter security fence.

LOUISIANA, BATON ROUGE

Albino dingo family in grotto: these should be neutered.

Hyena grotto inadequate and hazardous to visitors.

Shelters were provided for every animal; while some may not look pleasing, they serve purpose for animal comfort.

A fine, simple flight cage is provided for several eagles—one of best seen.

LOUISIANA, MONROE

Most cages larger than average, except cat pens which also have 90-degree corners. Cats appear in good condition, but overweight.

Grass-floored elephant and hippo exhibits are rare and good.

Large aviary (75 foot diameter) gives plenty of circular flight space. Entrance arrangement, however, is on inside of circle, which lessens flight area and is hazardous during panic.

LOUISIANA, NEW ORLEANS

Public feeding popcorn, etc. to otters—stools were loose and grey.

Most hooved stock overweight—especially cebu cattle trio. Rusty hogwire enclosures for cattle.

Flooded dirt floors in ungulate pens. Poor maintenance generally: odors and dirty.

Overweight jaguar with stereotype movement.

Lion's head has untreated wounds; cages rusty, dirty at 3:00 P.M.

Orangs' cage small and dirty.

Sea lions are in fresh water pool outside zoo fence.

Director Moore removed heating from cat cages.

Monkey cages dirty and in need of paint.

MARYLAND, BALTIMORE

Poor inside bird exhibit: glass telephone booth design with no sun and little light. Birds' feathers in poor condition.

Spikes in Kodiak bear cage at four foot level (keeper said: "to stop it climbing"), hazardous to animal and unsightly.

Many photos and expressions of self-praise of Mr. Watson and society. Staff had little respect for Watson—had little help with housing problems.

Many cage floors decaying, and much algae (keeper using ferrets for control of large rat population).

No heat in many cages—baboons with frostbitten tails and hands on exhibit.

All inside access doors closed during day. Very cold.

Public feeding encouraged—keepers watched while visitors fed everything.

Very overweight jaguar and two cubs; fat sloth and sun bears; fat leopards next to jaguars (we were shown around by fat keeper).

Zoo society members and keepers attempting to remove capture-gun dart from female buffalo that had been shot with antibiotic for a "cold" after losing calf; people were unfamiliar with this work—dangerous and ridiculous spectacle.

Mammal house is large ape jail.

Polar bear pool drain too small; pool dirty, shelter rat-infested.

MARYLAND, SALISBURY

Small, clean zoo; well presented and in most cases shows consideration for animals.

Unusually good jaguar cage provided with shrubbery on three sides; grass floor.

Small cat exhibit good.

Feeding is not allowed; no vending machines in zoo.

Heat lamps used in small shelters can be burn hazard.

MASSACHUSETTS, ATTELBORO

No perimeter fence—dogs roaming in zoo.

Excess food in gibbon cage; floor filthy.

Emus, buffalo, axis deer on mud, temperature 25°.

Bicycle riding allowed in zoo—saw no keepers or zoo staff (5:30 P.M.).

Polar and Himalayan bears' cages dirty—beer can in one.

MASSACHUSETTS, BOSTON
Franklin Park

Ungulate pens had acute angled corners. One pronghorn with badly deformed mouth and horn (untreated fracture of jaw) from trauma (keeper). Poor surface; rocky, sharp stones and dirt.

Zoo in process of renovation.

MASSACHUSETTS, SPRINGFIELD

Very old, dirty indoor building housing lions, monkeys, etc.; buffalo heads on wall; strong odor.

Indian elephant is chained in for entire winter on a 5-foot chain; electric fittings had been pulled down by her and not replaced.

Polar bear had bullet in head from police: it was shot when visitor put arm in cage, and suffers attacks frequently when wound infects (zoo society).

Buffalo was "tranquilized" by capture-gun, fell down steep bank, and lay for three days with broken leg (zoo society).

Local firework display ten yards from ungulates' pen on each 4th of July.

Tranquilized apes with capture-gun while on 6-foot shelves; apes fell to floor with some injuries.

MASSACHUSETTS, STONEHAM

Seals in fresh water dough-boy type pool. No provision for salt water filtration. Glass barrier too low—children can climb into pool.

Ape cages barren; need cleaning.

Stained glass effect in walk-through aviary detracts from birds; interior should be opaque white surface. Birds in lower part are in mud with strong mildew odor.

MICHIGAN, LANSING

Tiger had rickets in front legs; rear end also not functioning properly.

Too much space for viewing—not enough for cats.

Chimp in dark 10' x 10' cage.

Bird house of small glass-fronted cubicles is unsuitable, difficult to clean. Bird house smelled strongly of paint.

Cute names for animals—Romeo and Juliet for lion duo (separated).

MINNESOTA, ST. PAUL

Primate exhibit (two immature gorillas) is not designed for animals—sunken view, elaborate shape, too small for animals when larger.

Penguins' inside house enables birds to sit on high perch/shelf with danger of falling to outer floor; very small area.

Winter storage under main building dark, difficult to clean, and damp, especially for young elephant.

Sea lions in small fresh water pool, indoors all winter.

Moose with glaucoma displayed on mud surface.

Dogs allowed inside zoo building. (Mountain lion skin on exhibit—animal died from distemper.)

Zupreme surplus in many cages P.M. & A.M.

Tortoise by inside door near radiator with sign "ride me." Fat lady riding tortoise.

Frequent minor vandalism (keeper).

Grizzly bear was tranquilized by gun for "possible broken leg." Mate became upset and had to be "calmed by dart." She fell through melting ice of pool and nearly drowned. Mate did not have fracture on x-ray after all—"Oh well, back to the moat." (newspaper article on bulletin board)

MISSISSIPPI, JACKSON

Too many "cute" houses, villages for animal shelters.

Sea lion pool did not have provision for salt filtration. Spiked fence dangerous to seals; basic sanitation faults cause odor.

Bengal tiger exhibit lacks floor space—much of its 200 square feet occupied by steps, ornament; inside floor slippery when wet.

Four eagles without side screen or shelter box; cage is 10' x 10' x 10'.

Simulated rock painting ineffective and expensive.

Lions' simulated rock exhibit falling apart.

All birds in open area badly pinioned—from elbow joint.

Emu in rain—access door to shelter closed.

MISSOURI, KANSAS CITY

Sea lions with bad eyes in fresh water; dirty; marshmallows and paper cups in pool. Public feeding of unwashed frozen fish. One adult male blind (glaucoma).

Four great anteaters on concrete floor; loose stools, surplus, poorly mixed food on floor. (No commercial blender used.)

New gibbon exhibit moat too shallow (1' 6").

Ape house is monument to architect—wasted space with usual small quarters in elaborate exterior.

Hippo haul-out access poor; water dirty.

MISSOURI, ST. LOUIS

Seals in fresh water (elephant, California); filtration (new) cannot handle saline. One curator says it's not necessary, but feels that freeze-branding the zoo's three seals for identification is a must.

Lion house quarters cramped and odorous (roccal is used in zoo for deodorant).

Young walrus pools small and unfiltered, but did have salt (animals were valuable).

Cheetah "survival center" gimmick: train runs around part of perimeter about 3 feet from animals.

MISSOURI, SPRINGFIELD

Cat and other cages dirty. Zoo generally run-down.

Keeper hosing tiger while talking to visitors.

Three-foot security rail around cages inadequate.

NEBRASKA, LINCOLN
Antelope Park

Anteater on concrete—stool bad, no blender for formula.

Capybara display small and unbiological; slick floor.

Supervisor/director ex-dog catcher for city. Keepers seemed good despite direction.

Large aviary/mammal cage has no retiring shelters; should be closed at one end.

NEBRASKA, OMAHA

No provision for saline, filtration, or chlorination in seal pool; difficult to clean, no water source provided inside pool area for washdown. Keepers used cattle prod for controlling animals.

Orang/gorilla indoor housing very dark. Orangs had no climbing facilities inside cage. Strong odor present indoors.

Noisy steam train runs through zoo: sable antelope, bontebok, ibex too close to train—were panicked each time train passed.

Hogwire fence for musk oxen inadequate in panic situation.

Sumatran male tiger crippled (juvenile malnutrition).

Small, dirty monkey cages in old part of zoo.

Too much motor traffic, equipment operating close to animals.

Male ibex with badly overgrown hooves was panicked into running 100 feet each time train passed.

Collection of trophies ("shot around the world") is exhibited next to director's office, and well housed.

Anteaters exhibited correctly here on grass.

Elephant security rail (on visitors' side) in bad repair.

NEW JERSEY, NEWARK
Turtleback

Unsuitable floor (large, sharp rocks) for hoofed stock and emus. Emus' shelter poor—step up; animals not using it.

Sea lions in highly chlorinated fresh water pool, octagonal shape.

Exhibits shaped to please child or childish: kookaburra housed in fiberglass pig.

Genets cramped in cage 3' x 3'.

Some bird exhibits without shelters.

NEW JERSEY, SCOTCH PLAINS

Generally dirty and poorly maintained; dumping ground for other zoo surplus. Signs say several animals were donated by Bronx Zoo, including Siberian tiger with cataract.

Barn owl housed in pen with alligator—bird cannot move from rock perch.

NEW MEXICO, CARLSBAD

Much of park copied from Arizona Desert Museum and without attention to details. Dens for raccoon, etc. had bright light operated by visitors which wakened sleeping animals.

Aviary had flapping canvas for screens, frightening birds; otherwise cages were open to elements. Perches too close to public for birds' comfort.

Accent on botanical aspect of park; cactus and other plants warmly covered for winter weather.

NEW MEXICO, ROSWELL

Inadequate housing for coatimundi, raccoon, and coyotes.

Screech owls and hawks had no overhead shelter or screening from wind or rain.

Lions grossly overweight; separated to prevent fighting.

Macaque with young in unheated cage—heat lamp goes on at 35° (keeper).

NEW YORK, BUFFALO

Bear exhibits were snow covered and filled with much excrement.

Binturongs without climbing branches or retiring shelter.

Nocturnal animals without shelters or boxes.

All cats sex-separated to stop breeding (keeper).

Sea lions in fresh water, not much haul-out space; public feeding. Shelter had see-through door. Harbor seals in shallow pool, fresh water (originally designed for beavers).

Elephant house cramped, with three animals.

Birds housed in minimal space—4' x 4', with glass front; no hiding places. Hornbills with single perch, no flight space.

Black leopards display nervous condition (pulling fur out).

Many spiked security fences on pens which are outmoded and dangerous.

Shelters placed on ground for golden eagles occupy much of exhibit space.

Another elephant foot trash can in assistant director's office.

NEW YORK, LITTLE FALLS
Southwick's Wild Animal Farm

Basically an animal holding compound; owner is animal dealer; expected shipment of thirty infant elephants from India.

Young Siberian tiger on chain outside house of caretaker.

Dead heron or stork in cats' cage.

NEW YORK, NEW YORK CITY
Bronx

Cats' housing in need of paint. Wash basins provided for drinking water unsightly, difficult to clean. Considerable odor inside. Cages were adequate otherwise.

Monkey house quarters cramped (5' x 4'), glass fronted.

Sea lion pool—no filtration or saline provision, spiked fence unsuitable for marine mammals.

World of Birds very good for occupants: flight space, planting, climate, etc.

Kodiak bear and red fox exhibit best in country; spacious and attractive.

Signing both informative and amusing.

Lions housed in functional and attractive open area just far enough away to preserve their beauty and size to visitors.

NEW YORK, ROCHESTER

Sea lions in fresh water. Fur on one missing from chlorine burns (new DE filter failure) (keeper).

Male orang in 6' x 12' cage.

Zebra pen was flooded.

Moose and caribou heads do not belong on indoor house wall.

Wolves snowy, wet floor covered with excrement.

Carnival rides do not belong in zoo.

NEW YORK, SYRACUSE

Four hamadryas baboons crowded in 8' x 8' cage.

Bald eagle in unsheltered cage in inclement weather.

Coyotes, wolves had no shelter or roof. Snow on floor of pen at least one foot deep.

Cat cages were uniform 8' x 10', not large but at least had tree trunks for change.

NORTH CAROLINA, WILMINGTON

Small private menagerie provides minimal space, facilities for animals. No sewage facilities—difficult to clean. Fortunately only large animals are leopard, sun bear, and lion (AAZPA member).

OHIO, CINCINNATI

Roadrunner behind glass on concrete—no shelter.

Gibbon island (SD Zoo copy) had unnecessary, costly bridge arrangement; visitors were no closer to apes than if bridge were omitted. Apparently no provision for pool cleaning—water dirty.

Indoor cat cages too small: two leopards in 9' x 4'; extensive use of bathroom tile poor.

Seals in light-colored pool; fresh water.

Tasmanian devil with stereotyped movement (turning circles) housed in small, light pen—this nocturnal animal should be in dark area with dirt floor.

Ape house full of vending machines, balloons, concessions—do not belong in zoo.

Nocturnal exhibits—small pens for all animals shown.

OHIO, COLUMBUS

Eagle exhibit "designed especially for eagles" is architectural monstrosity with 3-inch metal perches for roosts.

Heavy algae in seal pool; fresh water; no filtration. One animal with chronic glaucoma, poor vocalization.

Indoor houses all dark and dirty; apes' new exhibit roof leaking badly.

OHIO, TOLEDO

Cheetahs in chain link run had no heat except two 250-watt heat lamps in roof of 6-foot metal shelter hut provided for birth of young (temperature was 0°.) (Keeper seemed quite proud of this.)

Anteater on concrete, glass-fronted exhibit.

Polished tile floors in glass-walled aviaries for storks, herons dangerous and unbiological.

Bear killed visitor in 1972—visitor in bear pen on day of visit: security faulty.

"Animal Care Center" housing chimps with diapers.

Surplus fish in seal pool; fresh water; algae.

New see-through exhibits are confusing. Dangerous restraint for ungulates: 2-foot ditch with rails on 6-inch centers with outline of jagged rocks.

Oklahoma, Oklahoma City

Two anteaters on concrete floor.

Sea lions in fresh water; surplus fish in pool.

Typical gorilla housing; one occupant vomited and reingested meal twice.

Best exhibits for dogs (wolves, dingos, etc.) we saw: grass, pools, trees, large area.

No staff visible when we left zoo at sunset.

Oklahoma, Tulsa

Hawks' shelters placed on ground.

Harbor seal in fresh water, indoors. Sea lions in fresh water; high chlorine content; one male blind.

Public able to surround cage housing screech owl.

Poor monkey exhibits; 6'x6' cells with tile.

Overhang on some moats (20-foot drop) hazardous.

Indigenous animal housing inadequate in size.

Small quarters and little shelter for ocelot, raccoon, and other small animals.

Skins of bobcat, coyote, and fox labeled "useful animals."

PENNSYLVANIA, ERIE

Sterile open-front gorilla exhibit with superfluous fiberglass decor in visitor's walkway.

Bear exhibits small; 10'x10' on concrete slope.

PENNSYLVANIA, NORRISTOWN

No security fence around zoo (neighbors don't want it); hole in fence of deer exhibit large enough for dog to get through.

Dirty water in sunbear's small cage.

New director wants to buld reptile house: perhaps a perimeter fence (less prestigious) would be more advantage.

PENNSYLVANIA, PHILADELPHIA

Mountain zebra with badly overgrown hooves; several other hoofed stock with same problem.

Cats in 10'x10' cages with no hiding place.

Dirty seal pool with fresh water; feeding platform with sign saying "Do not feed"; water full of pencils, paper, etc.

Nocturnal exhibits cramped.

Safeway store ape cages; area for animals small, 12'x10' with stone shelf and metal bar.

Mongoose lemurs in small glass-fronted pen without retiring space.

Tigers had large, moated outdoor area with chain link for easy egress from pool.

PENNSYLVANIA, PITTSBURGH

Squirrel monkeys, deer, lorikeets in dark, nocturnal show: "Twilight Zoo" poor copy of Bronx's.

Bear pens with much algae; bear food surplus.

Overweight cheetah surrounded by Zupreme.

Crippled tiger moved with difficulty.

Very dirty seal pool, completely green with algae; rocks also algae covered.

Monkey house dark (illumination from two 40-watt bulbs); orangs in 72 square foot cage, bars on 2 inch centers.

Penguins' water supply needs filtration or increased water flow; water very dirty.

Foxes, lynx cages full of excrement. Most exhibits dirty, need cleaning.

PENNSYLVANIA, SCRANTON

Leopard locked outside with frozen drinking water.

Mountain lion, other cats underweight; probably parasitic.

Eye problems with fallow deer; deer have poor shelter.

No staff seen during visit.

Cat cages small; 8'x10'.

RHODE ISLAND, PAWTUCKET

No perimeter fence. Polar bears outside main zoo, no security.

Every pen full of sleet/rainwater. Coyotes, raccoons standing in water with wet shelters. Mountain lion in four inches of water/mud (10'x6' cage).

Two sea lions indoors; fresh water. Outside pool filthy, probably not in use.

Zoo is case for local SPCA groups.

SOUTH CAROLINA, CHARLESTON
Animal Forest

Very attractive and well-designed park housing only indigenous animals.

Good natural outside exhibits for bobcats, mountain lion, black bear, and alligator, plus large aviary for indigenous birds. All exhibits made from existing forest.

SOUTH CAROLINA, CHARLESTON
Hampton Park

Zoo apparently being phased out—keeper wasn't sure. Remaining animals in poor condition. Vandalism high.

SOUTH DAKOTA, SIOUX FALLS

Fox and raccoon cages inadequate size.

Drinking water dirty in many exhibits.

Security fence at zebra exhibit too low—2'6'', danger of people falling in.

No staff present anywhere, not even to take our money (50¢ piece turnstiles).

Dangerous corners in concrete pen for pronghorns.

TENNESSEE, MEMPHIS

Cat house very dirty (cobwebs, excrement, etc.) and dark.

Similar restraint for ungulates as in Toledo; very dangerous.

Ape indoor house—typically sterile, glass-fronted.

TEXAS, ABILENE

Metal sleeping drums for tropical animals unsuitable (temperature 30°).

Bengal tiger and lions locked out of shelters—no windbreak outside.

Five sea lions in dirty fresh water; eyes bad. (Each gets two salt pills daily to make up for lack of salt water.)

No night security—some vandalism.

Sloth bears in bad condition; bloody stools.

Slick floor inside giraffe quarters; one suffered broken neck.

Ground hornbill had escaped from giraffe exhibit.

TEXAS, BROWNSVILLE

Anteaters on concrete; feet mutilated from rough surface.

Water moats hazardous; dirty.

Seal pool has fresh water, dirty. Seals suffering photophobia.

Lions' indoor housing has many internal extrusions, damaging one animals's head.

TEXAS, DALLAS

Deformed cassowary on exhibit.

Alligators in unheated pool with running water to prevent ice formation.

Camel on exhibit with front leg/foot lame.

Echidnas on hardwood floor; no cover.

Three fat Siberian tigers; Zupreme left over in every cat cage.

Antique bear pen with spikes should be junked.

Poorly built small bird pens for pheasants.

Birds' inside exhibit lacks sunlight or substitute.

Hoofed stock exhibits had bad corners in many pens.

Large mammal building is oversized supermart meat display: hippos, giraffes, and elephants are successfully hidden from visitor behind fogged windows.

TEXAS, EL PASO

Aviary unheated/uncovered.

Three seals died in one year; one from broken neck while being restrained.

Moving techniques poor; no tranquilizers used. Vet on call is local meat inspector.

Very high mortality on reptiles.

Pens with hoofed stock had bad corners. Keeper installed windbreak which has to be removed when important visitors are shown around (director's orders).

Primate house contains small cages (6'x6'x6') with several species of monkey; guenons displayed stereotyped movements. Visitors have more room than occupants.

TEXAS, FORT WORTH

Zupreme leftovers in many cages; Siberian tiger vomited (more Zupreme) twice while we watched.

No shelter or windscreen for eagles.

Harbor seal and Californian sea lion in fresh water; eyes bad.

Tiger exhibit space taken up largely by pool. Floor uneven; difficult to maintain.

Gorilla and orang exhibits poor—cramped.

Many exhibits run-down, need paint.

Director's office decorated with lion head and skin rug, elephant tusks, and warthog head.

TEXAS, HOUSTON

Tamandua on concrete; pacing.

Binturongs behind glass; hyperventilating (temperature 80°).

Sea lions in fresh water, poor vocalization.

Many rejected babies in nursery: five tigers, siamang, margay. Says little for husbandry (if indeed these are rejected), which may be cause of rejection.

Row of bird cages; some too low (8 feet) for animals—king vultures, eagles, etc.

Primate housing is sterile row of cubicles.

TEXAS, MIDLAND

Four golden eagles with Harris's hawks in exposed, uncovered cage.

Pregnant tiger carrying yesterday's meat—too fat to eat it. (Director asked for advice on pre-natal care.)

Coyotes in 10x4'x6' cage.

Small mammals have inadequate open box shelters; barn owls especially.

TEXAS, NEW BRAUFELS
Snake Farm

Buffalo and Texas longhorn cattle in filthy exhibit.

Adult chimp in small cage (3'x6'x10'); neurotic.

Sign asks visitors not to spit into exhibits.

Complete absence of trained personnel.

TEXAS, SAN ANTONIO

Two echidnas on concrete with some straw and two 250-watt heat lamps 6 feet from floor for warmth.

Fruit bats heated by heat lamps; burn hazard.

Female Californian sea lion sick but doing seal show.

Feeding machines throughout zoo; Himalayan bears grossly overweight; food everywhere.

Director and secretary had many zoo trophies on office walls. Zoo board room full of stuffed animals.

Gorilla's 8'x6' cell has 3/4-inch bars on 3-inch centers, plus glass front; occupants almost invisible.

TEXAS, TEXARKANA

Security fence only 4 feet high—frequent vandalism.

Female lion had rickets—can't walk or lift head above shoulder. Several other cats mutilated, i.e. bobtailed, etc.

Donation box for "feeding animals."

TEXAS, WACO

Dog runs for lions, coyotes, etc.—too small.

Jaguar with chronic bone malformation; walking with difficulty.

No security provided after zoo closing time.

UTAH, SALT LAKE CITY

Very dirty grounds; trash everywhere, including animal exhibits: capybara eating foil, paper.

Old inner house with elephant, sun bear, etc., very dirty. Sun bear in dangerously flimsy cage, patched up with baling wire.

Macaw in glass-fronted pen, floor heater (electric) in exhibit with standard rubber cord to outlet.

Woolly monkey convulsing on monkey island being dragged by spider monkey roommate. No keepers present (one reading paper in elephant house).

Zebras' hooves badly overgrown.

Seven mountain lions crowded in one exhibit.

Nocturnal animals (cacomistles, etc.) on concrete- floored exhibit without hiding places.

Poster depicting crossbred lion/tiger in cat house. Other signs say "do not throw anything in exhibits but clean food."

Sea lions in fresh water.

Ape exhibit housing hairless orangs; faulty surface on floor, walls.

Penguin pool classic of poor design: dark, small, no haul-out area (signs read "do not push penguins into water").

Poor distribution of space in cat house: 50 percent for public walkway.

Split-level giraffe exhibit poor: can only view head or feet close up.

Anteaters on grass—surprisingly.

VIRGINIA, NORFOLK

Sea lion in fresh, unfiltered water.

Lions, tigers overweight.

Feeding ducks, geese from one exhibit to raptors in next exhibit.

Chimp quarters too small for adult occupant.

WISCONSIN, MADISON

Combination seal and monkey island poor; water full of brown algae.

Penguins also in dirty, brown water.

No perimeter fence; zoo is not separated from houses or streets of city.

Hornbill behind glass; small cage.

Tiger cages cramped, 10' x 12' for two Siberians (these are rotated daily with lions in outdoor area). Indoor house odorous.

WISCONSIN, MILWAUKEE

Seals in fresh water; new exhibit has no provision for salt.

Outdoor exhibits large and well planned; most on grass or dirt.

Small mammal house had some unique see-through exhibits which looked out on wooded area.

WISCONSIN, RACINE

No security fence; neighbors objected. Ducks speared with sticks by vandals.

Aoudads' hooves badly overgrown—could hardly walk.

Sea lions in fresh water; vomited fish. Vandalized often (poisoned, stoned to death).

Chimps housed behind glass (cracked) in dark indoor house with cats and other monkeys (10'x10' pens).

APPENDIX II
MINIMUM REQUIREMENTS FOR CAPTIVE ANIMALS

ANTHROPOIDS

Exhibits should give adequate movement for animals, both lateral and vertical.

Organic material for climbing should be provided for great apes (heavy rope, tree trunks, etc.). Animals should be able to move freely (climb) over entire length of exhibit.

Smooth tile floor surface should not be used, nor fiberglass. Concrete floors should be easily drained, heated automatically, and have nonskid surface. Grass preferred.

Animals should be provided with therapeutic materials suited to their intelligence.

Bars, if used, should be spaced to give animals sufficient room to pass entire hand and forearm, with accompanying safety distance between bars and attendants' passage.

Bars or any metal surface must be painted or coated with materials considered nontoxic to humans.

Sunlight or automatically timed U/V artificial light must be available.

Retiring space should be available at all times. Organic surface must be provided on sleeping area. This should be in form of nest—not shelf without hand-hold for animal.

Space requirements minimum 25'x25'x15' high.

Viewing should not be from more than two sides.

SMALL MAMMALS, ACTIVE

Surface of at least part of exhibit should be wood or tree trunks.

Heat incorporated into floor of exhibit (controlled automatically) is necessary.

Climbing branches should be available for animals' use. Pool for bathing/drinking with cleaning facility should also be incorporated.

Size of exhibit should be determined by animal's size—minimum six times animal's length nose to tail/rear.

Retiring quarters above floor level should be available with access at all times.

Subdued light for nocturnals with additional hiding screens.

Additional quarters provided for multiple animal exhibits.

Viewing should be from no more than two sides.

Sunlight or U/V light must be available.

SMALL MAMMALS, INACTIVE

Climbing branches should be provided.

Retiring space with access at all times.

Space or infra-red radiant heat panels installed—no heat lamps.

Floor should be or organic material or heated concrete.

Pool for bathing/defecation included.

Subdued light for nocturnal species.

Viewing from no more than two sides.

Flying mammals need organic roost perch and flying space for exercise.

Sunlight or U/V light available daily.

GREAT ANTEATERS, AARDVARK

Earth or grass exhibit surface.

Access to heated retiring quarters at all times.

Large tree trunks for climbing.

Surface area minimum 30'x30'.

Adequate drainage during inclement weather.

Access to sunlight or U/V light.

TAMANDUA, PANGOLIN, ECHIDNA

Same requirements as first three for anteaters.

Surface dimension minimum 10'x10'x15' high.

Pool for washing/drinking.

Humidifying devices for dry heat (90°).

Viewing should not be from more than two sides.

(These animals are nocturnal.)

FELINES

Adequate area for movement—minimum 25'x25'.

Grass floor or nonslip concrete border.

Retiring shelter with auto heat accessible at all times.

Pool for drinking, bathing (tiger, leopard, jaguar).

Bars or mesh minimum 5'' centers.

Access to sunlight or automatically timed U/V light.

Climbing device—shelf (wood) or tree trunks.

Hiding space other than sleeping quarters.

Separate sleeping quarters if more than one cat.

Humidifiers for dry heat (80°).

Viewing must not be all around—only front and half of sides.

CANINES

Turf or dirt surface; area minimum 20'x50'.

Retiring shelter and heat access at all times.

Hiding places in exhibit.

Pool for drinking/bathing.

Humidifiers for dry heat (80° +).

One shelter per animal provided in multi-animal exhibits.

Access to sunlight or artificial U/V.

Viewing from maximum two sides of exihibit.

URSINES

Minimum space for large bears (Alaskan, brown, grizzly, polar, European) 30'x25'x20' high. Medium (sloth, Himalayan) 20'x20'x15' high.

Pools for Alaskan/polar bears large enough for swimming—others large enough for bathing.

Sun bears, smaller bears require climbing facility and access to dry-heated quarters.

Humidifiers for dry heat (80° +). Access to sunlight or U/V.

Requiring quarters with organic (wood) floors or heated concrete, with access at all times.

Viewing from maximum two sides.

Pinnipeds

Filtered salt water necessary.

Dark color concrete for pool.

Adequate haul-out access, depending on species.

Source of high-quality frozen or fresh fish, with seasonal change. (Herring, sea smelt, anchovy, mackerel, needlefish, rock cod, etc.)

Multi-vitamin/mineral supplement daily. Measured ration of food fed by hand individually.

Limit minimum temperature of water to 45°.

Provision of humidifying nozzles at pool area for use in hot (above 80°) weather.

Sand surface or grass for other than otaridae to allow movement without body/skin damage.

Pool should have no corners; minimum depth should be twice length of largest animal; curved grade at rim provided for phocidae haul-out.

Provision of shade from sun/inclement weather.

Aquatic Mammals

Pool for swimming/bathing with water change facilities.

Surface turf or smooth concrete.

Hiding place and sleeping quarters with free access.

Heat in floor or duck board for fur drainage.

Dimension of exhibit to allow for activity.

Gnawing material (trees, etc.) for rodents requiring it.

Shelter from rain and sunlight.

Humidifier for dry heat periods (85°).

UNGULATES

Humidifying devices for dry heat (80°).

Surface should be sufficiently abrasive to control hoof growth. If turfed, abrasive perimeter provided.

Area should allow ample movement for animals: length of animal x 10^2.

Exhibit corner boundaries must be radiused, not 90-degree corners.

Shelter from sun and inclement weather with heated floor available, also means of separation of animals in emergency.

Drainage should prevent flooding of exhibit surface.

Exhibit area should be free from projections or objects which might be hazardous to animals in panic situation. Concrete, solid walls should have radiused corners.

Restraining fence should not be hazardous to animals in panic situation. Moats should have suitable egress provision for any animal accidentally falling into water-filled moats.

Dry moats should have layer of straw sufficient to absorb shock in case of fall, plus egress for such emergency.

Negative overhang of exhibit floor surface over moat whether wet or dry is necessary.

Viewing from not more than two sides.

Pachyderms

Surface of pen turf or decomposed granite.

Access to heated quarters at all times.

Rubbing posts in outside and inside quarters.

Nonslip surface for floor of inside quarters.

Restraint by means of railing, bars which do not cause injury to skin from friction. No internal spikes or extrusions.

Access to U/V light where animals are inside for periods in excess of one month continually.

Drainage of both areas to be adequate in keeping floor dry. Surface of inside quarters should incorporate heat.

Size of area sufficient to allow animal exercise to assist in keeping feet in good condition. Minimum of six times animal's body length.

Dry moats should be padded with straw bales for emergency.

Water moats should be no deeper than animal.

Humidifying devices installed for dry heat (85°).

Viewing from three sides maximum.

Birds

Flight space for flying birds sufficient to allow minimal ten seconds' free flight between roosting perches.

Heat (infra-red, radiant) available at highest perches to allow all occupants access at all times, thermostatically controlled.

Humidifying equipment for dry heat (80°).

Minimum two perches to allow choice of roosting place in pecking order.

Pool for bathing or drinking (0''–6'' depth).

Free choice of hiding places (shrubs, screens, etc.).

Screening from weather and drafts.

Absence of loud noise (rides, raucous music) in vicinity of exhibit.

Roof for rain/sun protection with access at all times.

Perches of organic material—not metal/plastic.

Roost boxes where indicated should be at high point in exhibit, not on floor.

Viewing two sides maximum.

RATITES

Floor surface grass or decomposed granite.

Access to heat (in floor) in sleeping/shelter at all times.

Pool for drinking/bathing.

Hiding places (shrubs, screens) available, free choice.

Minimal size of exhibit: length of body x 10^2.

Sunlight available or U/V light in winter.

Viewing two sides maximum.

NOTES

1. John Perry, *The World's a Zoo* (New York: Dodd, Mead & Co., 1969).
2. *San Diego Wild Animal Park Wild World of Animals* (Zoological Society of San Diego, Inc., 1973).
3. *San Diego Wild Animal Park* (folder).
4. *World Wildlife Safari* (brochure).
5. *San Diego Wild Animal Park* (folder).
6. *San Diego Zoo* (flier).
7. "A New Experience," *San Diego Wild Animal Park Wild World of Animals* (Zoological Society of San Diego, Inc., 1973), p. 1.
8. *Topeka Zoo Guide Book* (Topeka Zoological Park, 1971), p. 43.
9. *Como Zoo Guide*, p. 3.
10. *Ibid.*, p. 4.
11. *Topeka Zoo Guide Book* (Topeka Zoological Park, 1971), p. 21.
12. *Arizoo*, Spring 1973 (Arizona Zoological Society), Vol. 2, No. 1, p. 10.
13. *Philadelphia Zoo Animal Book and Guide to the Garden,* second printing 1967 (Zoological Society of Philadelphia, 1964), cover page.
14. *Ibid.*, p. 17.

15. *Como Zoo Guide*, pp. 7, 9, 10.
16. *Fort Lauderdale's Ocean World* (brochure).
17. *Miami Seaquarium* (brochure).
18. *Sea World* (brochure).
19. *Marine World Goes Wild!* (brochure).
20. Frederick J. Zeehandler and P. Sarnoff, *Zeebongo: The Wacky Wild Animal Business* (Englewood Cliffs, N.J.: Prentice-Hall, Inc., 1971).
21. Barbara Harrison, *Orang-utan* (Garden City, N.Y.: Doubleday & Company, Inc., 1963), p. 170.
22. Information supplied by the New Mexico Fish and Game Department and Wildlife Conservation Coalition.
23. Jean Bausch, "Ordeal of Animals in Zoo Ends!" (Golden State Humane Society, October 1973).
24. "Death in the Zoo: Yes or No" (United Action for Animals, Inc., 509 Fifth Avenue, New York, N.Y. 10017).
25. "Zoo Animals on Brink of Disaster" (United Action for Animals, Inc.), p. 1.
26. Marlene Cimons, "It's Not Easy to Deceive a Grebe," *TV Guide,* October 26, 1974, p. 29.
27. *Ibid.*, p. 31.
28. Paul N. Linger, "Management of Captive Cats," *The Zoo Review* (Denver Zoological Foundation, Inc.), December 1972, pp. 5, 6.
29. Information supplied by cat keeper in Birmingham Zoo, February 1974.
30. Gerald Iles, *At Home in the Zoo* (London: W. H. Allen, 1960), p. 242.
31. *Humane Society of the United States* (bulletin).
32. "Stolen Animal Survey," *AAZPA Newsletter*, Vol. 16, No. 2, February 1975, p. 9.
33. *San Jose Mercury*, October 19, 1973.
34. Betty Ulius, "Rosalie Reed: In Transition,"*Playgirl*, Vol. 2, No. 7, December 1974, p. 15.
35. "Torment, Torture and Terror Close in on Zoo Animals" (United Action for Animals, Inc.), pp. 6, 7.
36. *Audubon Park Commission Report*, New Orleans, January 1, 1974, p. 22.

37. *Cheyenne Mountain Zoological Park Annual Report 1969*, Colorado Springs, Colorado, pp. 32, 33.
38. "Mammal Losses," *Zoological Society of Buffalo Annual Report*, December 31, 1973, pp. 27, 28.
39. John Burks, "Keepers Quit, Call S.F. Zoo 'A Real Mess,' " *San Francisco Examiner*, July 7, 1972.
40. H. Hediger, *Wild Animals in Captivity: An Outline of the Biology of Zoological Gardens* (New York: Dover Publications, Inc., 1964), from 1950 ed.
41. Marvin Jones, "San Jose, America's Cleanest Zoo," *International Zoo News*, Ed. Zeist, Holland.
42. Robert Wagner, "The Director's Report," *Jackson Zoological Park Annual Report and Inventory 1972–1973*, p. 2.
43. *Amusement Business News*, July 27, 1974.
44. "Time Runs Out for Zoo Animals" (United Action for Animals, Inc.), p. 3.
45. "Special Report on Zoos" (Humane Society of the United States, July 1972).
46. "Special Report on Zoo Reform" (Humane Society of the United States, March 1975).
47. *Ibid.*, p. 3.
48. *Philadelphia Inquirer*, August 25, 1974.
49. "Special Report on Zoo Reform" (Humane Society of the United States, March 1975), p. 3.

INDEX

Page numbers for illustrations are in *italic*.